Nicole's book Hush *is honest and takes a much-needed look at an issue that has been quiet for far too long. I know so many people will benefit from reading this book.*

~ Craig Gross,
Founder of XXXchurch.com

For those who are searching for hope and help, Nicole gently leads them to the only true Source of Healing, the Lord Jesus Christ. Her life story and the message of this book accentuate how someone's courage, honesty, forgiveness, and trust—as well as counseling and close relationships—all have their place along the journey. Nicole uses her story and the accounts of others she has met along the way to weave together insights of how God reaches into places where the deepest, darkest secrets are hidden and says, "You no longer have to hush." This is a well-balanced and sensitively written resource for survivors and those who want to help them.

~ Dr. Edee Schulze,
Dean of Student Life, Wheaton College

For over 30 years I have worked with many people, from child molesters to survivors to victims of priest/clergy abuse most recently. And still I wonder and ask why the Christian community is so reluctant to address this profound need in our world. What Nicole Braddock Bromley does for survivors of childhood sexual abuse in Hush *is what Jesus Himself did for the mute—gives them back their voice. Her courage and honesty that flow from these pages provide hope for God's hurting and wounded children. Nicole's insights on spiritual healing reveal a wisdom far beyond her years.*

~ Victoria Kepler Didato,
Director of Child Sexual Abuse Institute of Ohio

Hush *is so much more than a compelling account of one woman's journey into wholeness. This book provides a genuine education for victims, their families, and those who want to help them.* Hush *is a model of healing as it frees the wounded of the stigmatization that so often comes with sexual abuse. The book effectively addresses issues of faith, of intimate relationships, and offers practical advice for those who want to tell someone about their victimization. This fine book debunks the false and danger-ous notion that abuse does not occur in Christian homes. I wish everyone would read this book!*

~ Elizabeth Dermody Leonard, PhD,
Professor of sociology, Vanguard University

Writing out of incredible authenticity, beautiful compassion, sensitivity and grace, Nicole gives damaged hearts and minds permission to find their voice and healing through her powerful words of hope and peace in Jesus Christ.

~ Ron Kopicko,
University Chaplain, Spring Arbor University

Nicole Bromley writes with a transparent, fearless, and poignant voice that encourages readers to break the silence of concealed abuse. Furthermore, she testifies that the lies and stings of past emotional wounds do not have to linger, but in the presence of Christ He does bring truth and comfort leading to abundant life and freedom. We can know Him personally and intimately in our pain. Her book is a convincing invitation to seek His face with all our hearts.

~ Wendy Bisset, MD,
Director / Family Physician, Wheaton College

Reading this book is an effective building block in lives ravaged by the effects of child abuse.

~ Diane Tesch,
Co-Founder of Royal Family Kids' Camps Inc.

With the saturation of pornographic images in our society, sexual abuse has become epidemic. Nicole gives us a very important tool, which will bring about changed lives each time the silence is broken. Her encouragement, wisdom, and love bring healing within reach, as she makes the connection America needs to hear!

~ Vickie Burress,
National Speaker and Victims Assistance Coordinator,
Citizens for Community Values

hush

MOVING FROM SILENCE TO HEALING
AFTER CHILDHOOD SEXUAL ABUSE

NICOLE BRADDOCK BROMLEY

MOODY PUBLISHERS

CHICAGO

All Scripture quotations, unless otherwise indicated, are taken from the *Holy Bible, New Living Translation,* copyright © 1996, 2004. Used by permission of Tyndale House Publishers, Inc., Wheaton Illinois 60189, U.S.A. All rights reserved.

Scripture quotations marked NIV are taken from the *Holy Bible, New International Version®.* NIV®. Copyright © 1973, 1978, 1984 by International Bible Society. Used by permission of Zondervan. All rights reserved.

Scripture quotations marked THE MESSAGE are from *The Message,* copyright © by Eugene H. Peterson 1993, 1994, 1995. Used by permission of NavPress Publishing Group.

Scripture quotations marked NKJV are taken from the *New King James Version.* Copyright © 1982 by Thomas Nelson, Inc. Used by permission. All rights reserved.

Cover design and image: Tim Green | The DesignWorks Group, Inc. | www.thedesignworksgroup.com

Interior design: Julia Ryan, www.designbyjulia.com

ISBN: 0-8024-4864-X
ISBN-13: 978-0-8024-4864-4

Library of Congress Cataloging-in-Publication Data

Bromley, Nicole Braddock.
  Hush : moving from silence to healing after childhood sexual abuse
/ Nicole Braddock Bromley.
     p. cm.
  ISBN 978-0-8024-4864-4
  1. Child sexual abuse--Religious aspects--Christianity. 2. Child
sexual abuse--Psychological aspects. 3. Adult child sexual abuse
victims--Rehabilitation. I. Title.
HV6570.B76 2007
362.76092--dc22
[B]

We hope you enjoy this book from Moody Publishers. Our goal is to provide high-quality, thought-provoking books and products that connect truth to your real needs and challenges. For more information on other books and products written and produced from a biblical perspective, go to www.moodypublishers. com or write to:

Moody Publishers
820 N. LaSalle Boulevard
Chicago, IL 60610

1 3 5 7 9 10 8 6 4 2

Printed in the United States of America

FOR ANY VICTIM OF ABUSE
WHOSE VOICE HAS EVER BEEN SILENCED
BY SOMEONE WHO SAID, "HUSH!"

CONTENTS

Heartfelt Thanks . . .

To Moody Publishers: For believing in me and my message and for the vision, faith, and commitment that turned my dream into reality. A special thank-you to Editorial Director Dave DeWit. Your heart is as genuine as they come, and your expertise and guidance during the entire process have made this a very positive experience. Also to Acquisitions Coordinator Tracey Shannon, for your hard work and enthusiasm for spreading my message and ministry through this book.

To Dr. Judith St. Pierre, my editor: For your wealth of wisdom, your steadfast commitment to reshape this book, and your willingness to teach me along the way. What a gifted woman you are!

To Dr. Carol "Q" Harding: For your friendship and for making the midnight phone call that sparked this publishing adventure.

To Rev. Cynthia Stiverson (aka Mom): For being the mother I wish every child could have. You not only believed me and protected me after I broke the silence, but also helped me pave a new path and taught me what I needed to know to be able to share this message with the world. You have prayed with me and supported me every step of the way. Mom, you rock! You'll always be my best friend and my greatest mentor.

To my two awesome dads: My father, Gary, for your unconditional love and constant support. You've always believed in me. My stepdad, Mark, for your amazing godly example, advice, love, and the major role you played in helping me trust again.

To Kathy, Amber, and Garrett: For your love and encouragement, and to Alicia, for giving me a deeper well from which to draw in writing this book.

To all those across the country who have encouraged and supported me and this book: For your prayers, without which no work like this can be accomplished. Thank you to the OneVOICE prayer and support team, with special thanks to Pastor Joe and Rachel Blevins, Erin George, Debbie Paxton, Elijah Smith, and Ron Kopicko.

To the many other special friends, teachers, coaches, pastors, mentors, and family members: For loving and accepting me throughout my healing journey and now in ministry.

To the many administrators, student development staff, and chaplains: For graciously allowing me to minister on your campuses in the past few years. Your students have made this book possible; it is for them.

To my husband, Matthew: For bringing resolution to my story. This book wouldn't be complete without you. Your unconditional love, understanding, and support are what I hope every little girl who has survived childhood sexual abuse will experience through her knight in shining armor. Your godly character is everything other men should strive for. You truly are God's greatest gift to me, and words can never fully express how thankful I am for you or how blessed I am to be your wife.

To my heavenly Father, God: For Your great faithfulness. Your promises are true. You have brought good out of bad; You have brought healing and given me hope and a future. May my life always reflect Your grace and love to those who silently hurt. This is Your book, Lord. Thank You for allowing me to be Your vessel.

OUR LITTLE SECRET

When my flight arrived on the West Coast for a college speaking engagement, a student named Shelby picked me up from the airport in her bright red Jeep Wrangler.

"Wow! Nice ride!" I said as I climbed in. "I couldn't afford anything like this when I was in college."

"I can't either," Shelby said. "My brother gave it to me. He didn't want it anymore."

"Why not?" I asked. "It's pretty sweet!"

"You'll see," Shelby said as she pulled onto the freeway.

As we headed for the campus, there was so much racket coming from under the hood that I was afraid the transmission was going to fall out.

"See what I mean?" Shelby asked. "This happens whenever I drive over fifty."

Above the noise, we chatted about what it is that I do. I told her about my organization, OneVOICE Enterprises. "VOICE is an acronym for 'Victory Over Impossible CircumstancEs,'" I explained. "I founded OneVOICE to raise awareness of and help prevent sexual abuse. I travel to schools, churches, and conferences across the country to talk about it. Most of the time I speak at Christian colleges."

"Christian colleges?" Shelby said. "I don't get it. I didn't think students at Christian colleges experienced anything bad like that."

Although Shelby's statement distressed me, it didn't surprise me. I've found that many people think sexual violence will never touch them or affect anyone close to them. Yet the reality is that sexual abuse takes place everywhere—even in respectable, loving, Christian families. It occurs where we least expect it, and it affects all of us.

As they travel the road of life, many abuse survivors are much like Shelby's car. From the outside, you would never guess that something is seriously wrong on the inside. I know, because I'm an abuse survivor whose life for many years wasn't all it appeared to be.

I'll never forget when my second grade teacher, Miss Maggie, conducted an informal survey among the members of our class. Afterward, she told my mother that I would be homecoming queen when I grew up. It seems ridiculous that Miss Maggie could predict who would be homecoming queen ten years later. But she was right. I was voted onto the homecoming court in my freshman, sophomore, and junior years, and when I was a senior, I was crowned homecoming queen.

Almost everyone who knew me considered me the "perfect girl" from the "perfect family." I came from a happy Christian home, and I excelled as an athlete, scholar, artist, and class leader. My life seemed ideal. But behind my bright hazel eyes, my superachiever persona was masking a Nicole who was hurting from childhood sexual abuse and afraid to tell her friends. My silence, like the silence of so many victims of abuse, helped hide the truth that sexual abuse is running rampant in our country.

Today, a shockingly high percentage of our nation's college and university students are silently struggling with the effects of childhood sexual abuse. In 2000, researchers at the National Center for Victims of Crime estimated that one in every three girls and one in every six boys are sexually abused by the time they turn eighteen. In 1996, the United States Department of Health and Human Services concluded that approximately 80 percent of sexually abused children know the perpetrator. In 30 to 50 percent of the cases, parents and other relatives are the offenders. I speak all over the United States, and I know that many people aren't even aware of these staggering statistics.

"Our Little Secret" is the title of the keynote speech I give across the nation. I chose this title because I believe that sexual abuse is the best-kept secret in our nation today. Most people fear this secret and prefer to sweep it under the rug so they won't have to deal with it. As a result, a dark cloud of silence—a "hush"—hangs over our communities, cloaking the truth.

I'm concerned about people who, like Shelby, are living in the midst of an abused and hurting generation, yet unaware that it exists. I'm concerned about people who, raised in the church, are sheltered from the painful realities of this world. I'm concerned about campuses, churches, and communities where people are afraid of being *real*.

One of the greatest privileges each of us has is the right to be heard. Yet I've met an incredible number of victims of sexual abuse whose stories have never been heard because they have never had a voice. I've written this book to give victims of abuse a voice and to raise other voices to support them.

As you read, you'll hear me talk about dark and light, lies and truth, bondage and freedom. If no one sheds light on what is being done in the darkness, it will never stop; and survivors will never know the truth that will set them free from the lies that keep them in bondage. Every time we bring abuse into the light, we help prevent more abuse while we help its victims heal.

Victims need their own voice to break free from their silent pain. But they also need your voice. They need my voice. Together, our voices become *one voice*, one that rings loud and clear as it speaks words of love and truth, of validation, acceptance, and comfort. Our voice will penetrate the darkness to expose sexual abuse for exactly what it is. Our voice will lead wounded hearts to a safe, open place of healing. And as we speak out, our voice will reduce the risk of abuse for the next child, and the next, and the next.

As you read my story and hear the voices of other victims of childhood sexual abuse, I pray that you will find your own voice. Silence protects the violators, not the victims. May the silence be broken.

AS I STOOD THERE IN SILENCE THE TURMOIL WITHIN ME GREW WORSE.
AS I STOOD THERE IN SILENCE THE TURMOIL WITHIN ME GREW WORSE.

AS I STOOD THERE IN SILENCE THE TURMOIL WITHIN ME GREW WORSE.

1

A LEGACY OF "HUSH"

Some of my early memories are very vivid. Even today, certain sounds or scents immediately transport me back to the picturesque setting of my childhood home. It stood

⟶

AS I STOOD
THERE IN
SILENCE
THE TURMOIL
WITHIN ME GREW WORSE.

Psalm 39:2

on a hill off an old country road in a small farm town in Ohio. I can still picture myself coming home after school, walking up the long lane to the white three-bedroom ranch-style house with blue shutters.

When I arrived, my crazy little dog, Frisbee, would get so excited he would jump all over me, while my more composed cat, Cotton, would rub against my legs, leaving a trail of white dander to blow in the wind and land on my clothes. Mom would be waiting for me at the sliding glass door of her sewing room, where she crafted dolls to sell at festivals and art shows. It was the perfect home for the perfect family.

THE PERFECT FAMILY

I was one of the few kids in my school lucky enough to have a "cool" mom. You know, the kind you don't mind being seen with in public, the kind who buys you clothes you'll actually wear. My mom was hip without even trying to be. It was just who she was. She looked cool. She dressed cool. She talked cool. She was smart and funny. My friends seemed to like hanging out with her almost as much as they did with me.

Mom was a great friend as well as an awesome mother. She was always there for me and always understanding, even when I made those dreaded phone calls from school to say I'd forgotten my basketball shoes or left my homework on the kitchen table. I felt I could talk to her about anything.

My parents divorced when I was only a year old, and my mother remarried when I was three. My stepfather, Vince, was a salesman, and every day he'd go out to scour the countryside for customers. I used to pretend I was going to work just as Daddy V did.

My mom would pack a lunch for me in a brown paper bag. I would kiss her good-bye and head out the kitchen door to the garage. I pretended that my truck was the old gray Ford tractor parked in the corner of the garage. I would climb up on the red metal seat and eat my lunch. I always told my mom not to look at me because, after all, I wasn't really there. I was driving to work! You can imagine how exciting it was when Vince let me sit on his lap and steer the tractor as he drove it around our property.

My mother and stepfather were attentive, loving parents. They were always there to tuck me into my soft pink bed at night, read me a bedtime story, and say a night-time prayer. They encouraged me to discover and pursue my talents, and I always knew they would support me in all my activities, which eventually included ballet, gymnastics, basketball, volleyball, track, and art.

Daddy V was always willing to spend time with me. I never felt like an unwanted stepchild. He treated me as if I were his own daughter. He was always there to push me on the swing or ride bikes down the road and back. When I wanted to play basketball, he dropped whatever he was doing to practice shooting with me. He encouraged me to work hard and play hard, and he was my biggest sports fan. I always knew that he believed in me, and that gave me the confidence to try anything.

This was Vince's second marriage as well, and his three children visited us frequently. Our healthy, loving relationships could have served as a model for other blended families. It was akin to *The Brady Bunch*—only without the maid! My stepsister Steph and I were the same age and best friends. She spent every weekend and most of the summer with us.

Of course there was also the extended family: grand-parents, aunts, uncles, cousins. Our house was where every-

BEHIND THE BLUE SHUTTERS one would gather whenever there was a reason to throw a party. The family album bulged with photos of the annual Fourth of July birthday party, where my cousin Mandy, my stepsister Crystal, and I were the guests of honor. At Christmas and sometimes at Easter, our home was the scene of two family dinners, one for each side of the family. The aroma of homemade rolls drifting from the oven, the taste of freshly baked pies, and the warmth of a close-knit family left everyone longing for the next occasion to make memories together.

When I was little, I wanted to know everything. I couldn't understand why I had to wait to know what everyone else already knew. When I was three, I begged Mom to teach me to read; she finally taught me when I was four. I couldn't figure out what the holdup was. Why did I have to wait so long?

I remember spending hours following along with the pages as I listened to books on tape. These weren't the ones you can find at the local library. These were homemade! Mom would record a cassette tape of herself reading one of my books, and when it was time to turn the page, she recorded herself ringing a bell. She must have been obsessed with bells, because she also had a dinner bell she rang every night to call us in to eat. I never knew whether it was time to read or time to eat!

In first grade, my teacher gave each student in our class a paper to fill out for our first visit to the library. It asked what kind of book we wanted. If we found it, we were to write down the title. I was looking for a book that would tell me "all the stuff that grown-ups know." After searching shelf after shelf for this book, I finally gave up and wrote, "They didn't have a book like that." At the bottom of the paper, my teacher wrote, "That's too bad!"

I now know that it was a good thing there wasn't a book like that. From all outward appearances, I had the perfect family and the perfect life. But behind the blue shutters of my perfect home, I was learning things no child should ever know.

I learned a lot from my stepfather. He told me how to build a bluebird house, but he also told me dirty jokes. He showed me how to use a clutch to shift, but he also showed me pornographic movies. He taught me how to grow a big vegetable garden, but he also taught me how to stimulate a man. He made me believe that it was safe to tell him anything, but he also made me believe that it was never safe to tell anyone "our little secret."

OUR LITTLE SECRET

As I grew, at times the memories of my stepfather's abuse had a dreamlike quality that made it difficult to know whether it really happened. Though some memories are still shrouded in clouds and mystery, I remember some events as clearly as if they happened yesterday.

One day when I came walking up the driveway after school, I didn't see Mom at the door. I remembered her telling me that she might be late because she had to go to town for groceries, so I headed to the big rock in one of our flower beds where the spare house key was hidden. As I bent over to move the rock, my stepfather came out of the house. I wasn't expecting him to be home early, so he startled me. He told me that the customer he had called on was working out in the fields, so he had decided to meet with him the next morning instead.

I went inside, plopped my books on the dining room table, and got myself a bowl of ice cream to eat while I did my homework. Vince wanted to play slapjack, my favorite card game. I was only in second grade and didn't have much homework to do, so I agreed to play. He wanted to make up a new rule and asked me to come up with one. I didn't have any ideas, so he said that whoever won a hand got to tickle the other person. I hated tickle games, but I loved playing slapjack.

Vince won the first hand. Then the second. And the third. The more he won, the more uncomfortable the tickling became. After the fifth game, he grabbed me from behind, pulled me onto his lap and put both of his hands on my chest. I tried to pull away, but he was strong, and he held me tighter. I screamed for him to stop. He laughed and said, "But I won! I get to tickle you until I'm done." Then he let go.

I didn't want to play anymore, but he said that if we played one more hand and I won, I could do my homework. He let me win the last one, but when I reached for my math book, he grabbed my hand and told me I had to tickle him. I didn't want to tickle him, and I barely touched him. I felt like throwing up.

Vince got mad at me and when Mom came home, he told her that I was acting cold toward him and that I'd hurt his feelings because he thought I would be excited that he was home early. Even though I hated the tickle game, he made me feel bad for pushing him away. I had wanted to tell Mom how I felt about the tickling, but not after what he told her.

I also clearly remember one night when I was about nine or so. For fun our family would throw empty aerosol cans into our outside firepit. (Obviously, there wasn't much to do in our small country town!) Then we'd run for cover and listen. Pretty soon we'd hear it—*pop!* One evening, Vince came into the house to tell me that he had some acrosol cans to throw into the firepit. Mom was working on her crafts, so I went outside alone with him. He gave me a can to throw, and as soon as I did, we ran as fast as we could into the woods behind our house.

Usually a can would pop in a matter of seconds, but this one didn't. Vince told me to sit down on the ground with him and wait. He sat behind me, with his legs on either side of me and his arms hugging my shoulders. We giggled and whispered, trying to be quiet enough to hear the pop. Still nothing. He kept talking about why it might take awhile for the can to get hot enough.

> HE TOLD ME THAT IT WAS OUR LITTLE SECRET.

At the same time he was whispering to me, his right hand was going down the front of my pants and into my underwear. I froze. He was touching me all over down there. I couldn't breathe. I prayed the can would pop so we could go inside the house. I tried to get up. He told me to sit still and enjoy it. I didn't enjoy it. I didn't even know what "it" was, but I wanted whatever it was to be over. I pushed his hand away.

He told me that it was our little secret.

As we walked back into the garage, he told me that it was our little secret and that if Mom ever knew what we did together, she would be very jealous. When we reached the steps leading into the house from the garage, he made me stand on the second step. Then he lifted my shirt and put his mouth on my breast. I felt so dirty. After forty seconds that seemed like an eternity, he reminded me how important it was for me to never tell. He said that if I told and Mom divorced him, it would be my fault and she would never want to see me again.

I turned around and walked into the house, acting as if nothing had happened. Vince came in a few minutes later, doing the same. But whenever he caught my eye, he would wink at me. That night my fear and confusion kept me from telling my mom, and because I kept silent, my stepfather continued to abuse me.

HUSH!

As a child, I believed that Vince loved me and that he would never mean to hurt me. Yet I still felt scared and confused, and I remember times when I wondered if what he was doing was wrong. He kept telling me that I was very special and that what he was doing was okay. He was my stepdad, and I trusted him. I also remember that whenever I became angry with him and pushed him away, he wouldn't talk to me for days. Sometimes it seemed that he was nice to me only before he molested me. Then he would say things like "If you love me, you'll let me." I did love him, and I didn't want to upset him or make him sad.

Vince was a very smart man. He was very careful about the kind of activities and groups we were involved in. Though we were Christians and committed to our faith, there was an unspoken law in our home that we weren't to go to church.

My mom became a Christian when she was eight years old, and my stepdad when he was a young adult. During his first marriage, Vince was a leader in his church. But after his divorce he felt a lot of shame and anger. I think he felt judged because of the divorce, so he basically abandoned the church community and tried to live the Christian life on his own.

While I was growing up, we were always conscious of God in our daily life. Our entire family belief system was based on the Bible. We applied it to our lives. We prayed together and tried to live a Christian life. Family friends and kids at school always considered my family Christians, and even as a little girl I was very conscientious about setting a Christlike example.

At the time, I was never sure why we didn't go to church, but looking back, it's clear that Vince considered church a safe place where our little secret might slip out. Unaware that he was abusing me, my mom went along because she didn't want to rock the boat. Vince directed every moment of her life. He guarded her time more closely than he did his own. She had to account for everywhere she went and how she spent every minute of her day. She felt as if she was always walking on eggshells around him, and she didn't want to do anything to disrupt what she and everybody else considered our perfect family life. Mom told me that there were times she wanted to tell him she was going to go to church on her own, but she was scared of how he would react.

Like my stepdad, abusers are characteristically con- trolling and overprotective not only of the child victim, but also of the nonoffending parent and anyone else in the child's circle who might one day spill the beans. They often isolate their victims to keep them from realizing that other families don't do these things.

My father, Gary, and my stepmother, Kathy, married when I was six. They have two children: my sister, Amber, and my brother, Garrett. I love them all dearly and enjoy spending time with them at their farm. However, that wasn't always the case.

When I was little, my stepdad often told me that my father was a bad dad and that he didn't really love me as much as I thought he did. He said that the custody rights could be changed when I turned twelve and that my father was going to try to take me away from my mom as soon as my birthday came. Vince did everything he could to make me think that my father didn't care as much about me as he did about getting back at my mom for their divorce. He tried to keep me from spending too much time with my father and made me feel guilty for wanting to go to his house. As I grew older, I began to accept these lies, just as I accepted his lies about the abuse.

One day when I was in fifth grade, the local sheriff deputy came to show our class a video. It was a cartoon. It might sound strange that she would come to a school library to watch cartoons with a bunch of ten-year-olds. But the cartoon wasn't really funny at all. It was about an uncle who took his nephew on a fishing trip. While they were in the boat, the uncle said strange things and touched his nephew in places that made the boy feel very uncomfortable. The deputy emphasized that what the uncle did was wrong. My stomach was tied up in knots. I felt uncomfortable and scared, just like the boy in the video. I really wanted to talk to somebody.

After the video ended, we lined up to go back to class. I cut to the front of the line and whispered to my teacher, Mrs. Webber, that I wanted to tell her something. But then I said, "I'll just wait and write about it during journal time on Wednesday."

When Wednesday rolled around, I wrote a poem about a bear named Mr. Stutter who liked peanut butter. It seemed obvious to me that Mr. Stutter had nothing to do with what I wanted to tell her, and I decided that if my secret was really that important, Mrs. Webber would follow up and ask me what I wanted to talk to her about. But weeks went by, and Mrs. Webber never asked. And I never told.

I remember feeling that I had no choice and no way to get out of my situation. I forced myself to believe that it wasn't that big of a deal. I would just have to suffer through it and not tell anyone. I thought I had to protect my mom and keep our perfect family together.

FROM LOOKING AT ME NO ONE WOULD EVER HAVE IMAGINED HOW MUCH TURMOIL WAS GOING ON INSIDE ME.

From looking at me, no one would ever have imagined how much turmoil was going on inside me. Nobody could have known that I was longing to be someone else, trying to figure out how I could run away from home, and sometimes even wishing my life would end. I was plagued with horrible nightmares, and I would often wake up crying. I was miserable, and I was scared.

Keeping silent was taking a terrible toll. Nevertheless, I thought I would have to live with this deep, dark secret for the rest of my life, for I was too afraid to tell.

WE HAVE MADE A LIE OUR REFUGE AND FALSEHOOD OUR HIDING PLACE.
WE HAVE MADE A LIE OUR REFUGE AND FALSEHOOD OUR HIDING PLACE.

WE HAVE MADE A LIE OUR REFUGE AND FALSEHOOD OUR HIDING PLACE.

2

THE LIE
THAT BINDS

Anna never received any attention from her family, or from anyone else, for that matter. So when her band director began saying nice things to her and keeping her after school to

———→

WE HAVE

MADE A LIE

OUR REFUGE

AND FALSEHOOD

OUR HIDING PLACE

Isaiah 28:15 NIV

help her learn new songs, she felt good inside. But when he made her give him oral sex during his free period, she knew something was wrong. She didn't want his attention anymore. She wanted out, but she was afraid to tell anyone because she believed that it was her fault and that everyone else would think so too.

Sexual abusers often convince their victims that the abuse was their own fault. To understand why Anna, I, and other survivors of abuse believe this lie, we have to go back to the day we were traumatized by sexual abuse, the day our little secret began.

PROGRAMMED FOR SILENCE

Sexual abuse is like a bolt of lightning that strikes us at our very core. It's more than an attack on our body; it's an assault on our emotions, mind, and spirit. Part of our being is completely frozen in that moment of betrayal, confusion, sadness, hurt, and shame. In some ways we develop as we should as we get older, but in one very deep and intimate area of our life, we always remain as we were in the attic with Dad when we were four, at the lake with Grampa when we were eight, or in the backseat of Coach's Jeep when we were twelve.

Those of us who were abused in childhood often believe things about ourselves that are completely false. Some of our beliefs were never true; they were lies when we were children, and they are lies now. Others were true for us at that particular time in that specific setting. Still others are the result of what our mind concluded must be true because of what was happening to us and around us.

Many times the lies we believe about ourselves come from the statements our abusers made to intimidate, belittle, or coerce us into doing something that would gratify their own evil desires. They persuaded us that we're alone—that no one else has experienced the same thing and that nobody will understand, support, or believe us. In our fear and despair, we accepted these lies as the truth. Some counselors refer to this as "programming." Whether deliberately or not, our abusers programmed our minds to believe certain things and respond in a particular way.

STUDENTS OFTEN ASK ME "IF I LET IT HAPPEN WASN'T IT MY FAULT?"

Even nonabusive adults can unintentionally program children to believe lies simply through their words and behavior. Children don't have enough experience to be able to distinguish between the truth and a lie. They want to believe that they are valuable and loved, but if they don't have that in their relationships, they don't really know any better. They are bound to their environment and have no choice but to trust the adults around them. They have to think, feel, and do as they are told.

Children also don't have the cognitive ability or emotional maturity to accurately assess what is happening to them. They can't make sense of what is being done to them other than to conclude that for some reason they themselves are to blame: They are bad; they are dirty; they are gross; they are stupid; they are weak. For a sexually abused child, these lies can seem unmistakably true.

Children are vulnerable, easily manipulated and controlled. Abusers know this and take advantage of it. They are often experts at what they do and can easily cement in their victim's mind the idea that what they are doing is actually "team-oriented." Constantly using the term "we," they send the message that if *we* are doing it, the child is somehow at fault.

Students often ask me, "If I let it happen, wasn't it my fault?" In all my travels and interactions with survivors, I've found this to be without a doubt the most common lie abuse survivors believe. When you peer into the dark world of sexual abuse, you can begin to understand why adult survivors have to struggle so hard to combat this belief. If it isn't exposed for the lie that it is, it will lead to other lies that prevent us from healing.

BOUND BY LIES

My stepfather made me feel that it was my choice to be abused. He made me believe that I deserved it and that I wanted it. He made me think that I could have stopped it if I had chosen to. All of these false beliefs are rooted in the biggest, fattest lie of all—that the abuse was my fault.

X Lie: I could have stopped it.

I can remember thinking, *If only I'd locked the bathroom door,* and *If only I hadn't offered to help him with outside chores at night.* I've heard others say things like *If only I'd worn long pajamas to bed instead of a nightshirt,* and *If only I'd yelled for help.*

Young children are self-focused and believe that the world revolves around them. They automatically assume that anything that happens in their world is the result of something they have or haven't done. It follows that if they did something to cause the abuse, they could do something to stop it, if they could just figure out what. Failing to stop it can lead to a tremendous amount of false guilt.

It's frightening for children to believe that they have no power over their body or their circumstances. Believing that they could have stopped it makes it seem as if they had some control. But that's a lie. A child is no match for a sexual predator and cannot stop the abuse from occurring.

Adult rape victims have similar false beliefs. They tell themselves: *If only I hadn't gone to that party . . . if only I hadn't answered the door . . . if only I hadn't gone back to his room . . . if only I hadn't been drinking.* Although as adults we do have more power to protect ourselves than children do, the fact is that we all find ourselves in situations where we are absolutely powerless to control what happens to us. "If only" statements like these just perpetuate the lie that the abuse was our fault.

If you're a survivor of childhood sexual abuse or rape, you were the victim. Period. No matter what you said, did, felt, wore, touched, drank, smoked, or where you went with whom, it was *not* your fault; and it's a lie that you could have stopped it. The abuser should have stopped it before it started. You never should have had to face the situation in the first place. You didn't start it, and you couldn't have stopped it.

✕ Lie: I wanted it.

Like many survivors I've talked with, I thought that being abused was my fault because I had somehow asked for it. This lie takes root when a victim feels physical pleasure during the act of abuse. If you can relate to this statement, you probably feel as if your body betrayed you.

The belief that I was to blame because there were times when my body felt good was one of the most difficult lies for me to overcome. I couldn't accept that my body could want anything so horrible. For years, I thought that if any of it made me feel good, I must have wanted it. Even in college, I struggled with this false belief because in the back of my mind, I knew that there were times when I probably did enjoy how it felt.

I will never forget the day I came to understand that our bodies are made to respond to touch. My body didn't betray me; it was doing what it was supposed to do! It just wasn't supposed to be awakened to touch in the way and at the time that it was. Once I accepted this truth, I was able to completely understand that *it was not my fault*! It was my stepfather's fault.

It's important to understand that your body's involuntary response to touch isn't the same as consent. You may have enjoyed the feeling, but you didn't enjoy being robbed of your innocence. You didn't enjoy having someone more powerful than you force his sin upon you. You didn't enjoy being abused.

X Lie: I'm responsible for my family's happiness.

Kelly's abuser was her dad's best friend, Don. She knew that her dad had no idea that his former college roommate had been sexually abusing her since she turned twelve. Don would come by the house when no one else was home and say that he was dropping something off her for dad or that he had left something in the garage and needed to pick it up. Once he got a foot in the door, he would harass her and eventually push her into sexual encounters. Kelly wanted to tell her parents, but she didn't want to ruin her dad's twenty-year friendship with Don. She felt responsible for keeping this secret in order to keep everyone happy.

Scott never told anyone that his Uncle Bill had been exposing himself to him since they went on their first annual camping trip when Scott was six. One time, Uncle Bill made Scott touch him. Scott thought it was weird and gross, but he was afraid that if he told, his uncle would lose his job as the Little League baseball coach. Baseball was his Uncle Bill's life, and Scott didn't want to make him unhappy by revealing this secret.

Just as Kelly and Scott weren't responsible for what their abusers chose to do, they weren't responsible for their abusers' happiness. Nor was it their responsibility to keep their abusers' friendships intact or reputation in place. They should never have been placed in this position. The abusers were the ones who placed their family or friendship or reputation in jeopardy, and *they* were responsible for the consequences of their actions.

YET IN ALL MY TRAVELS, I HAVEN'T SPOKEN TO A SINGLE STUDENT WHO WAS NOT, AT ONE TIME OR ANOTHER, AFRAID TO TELL.

All of these lies are common to the young men and women I've spent time listening to, talking with, and praying for; and all stem from the belief that the abuse was our fault. They are the result of the trauma and pain of sexual abuse, and they imprison us in a false belief system that makes us afraid to tell.

As I've traveled extensively over the last several years, I've seen firsthand the impact of abuse on survivors of all ages, races, backgrounds, and faiths. Yet in all my travels, I haven't spoken to a single student who was not, at one time or another, afraid to tell. Identifying the lies that fuel our fears can help us find the courage to tell. Why are we afraid to tell?

I'm afraid nobody will believe me.

The fear of not being believed keeps many victims from telling their secret. My stepfather told me that no one would ever believe me because he was a well-respected adult, while I was just a little girl. It made sense to me that everyone would believe him instead of me; I never questioned it.

Victims of abuse should be believed, but sadly, that often isn't the case. Most of the time when a child tells, nothing happens. The media often report on victims who come forward, only to have their case go nowhere and the perpetrator go free. This is a common, heart-wrenching theme in the stories I hear from survivors all over America.

Jessie told me that her father raped her continuously for about four years. She lived in fear and slept with the light on every night. She hated it when her mother had to work late, because her dad would force her to watch pornographic videos and imitate what she saw. One day she finally found the courage to tell her mother. She was scared that it would hurt her mom, but she hoped her mother would protect her from being abused again.

Unfortunately, Jessie's mom betrayed her trust and dashed her hopes. Instead of believing her, she chose to side with Jessie's father. She called Jessie a liar and told her never to tell anyone else.

What Jessie couldn't have known was that her mother was a victim of childhood abuse who had never dealt with it in her own life. She was afraid to acknowledge her daughter's pain for fear it would force her to face her own awful memories. And because of her low self-esteem, she dreaded the emotional and financial repercussions of losing her husband. Not wanting to face the truth, she refused to believe that he would do such a thing and chose not to believe Jessie. Her denial crushed all the courage it had taken for Jessie to tell her secret.

Remember that most of the world knows little about sexual abuse. People who are ignorant about the issue don't know how to respond appropriately. It's also possible that someone you trust may have some unaddressed pain in her past that you, like Jessie, know nothing about. Even a nonabusing parent with no history of abuse can be torn between the truth of her spouse's horrific acts and her love for him. This means that many times the response of the person you tell your secret to won't be what you need and deserve to hear. Sadly, sometimes the person you tell simply isn't prepared to hear your story.

I'm sorry if someone you thought you could trust with something so personal made you think you were bad, wrong, gross, or stupid. You should never feel this way. Those feelings are meant for the one who brought you pain. Whether the world is prepared to hear your story or not, the bottom line is that you deserve to be believed.

The bottom line is that you deserve to be believed.

I'm afraid something worse will happen.

Sexual abusers often tell their victims that if their secret gets out, bad things will happen. This fear is very real for abuse victims, and the perpetrators will use it to keep us silent. They will often threaten to harm us or those we love.

My stepfather told me that my mom would be jealous of his relationship with me, that she would hate me, and that I would never see her again. He said that if I ever told, the police would take me from her and send me to live with people I didn't even know. I would lose my family and never see them again. He also said he would kill my dog, Frisbee.

Ruth's big brother, Todd, told her repeatedly that if anyone ever learned about their secret, he would do the same thing to her three-year-old sister. Ruth felt she would rather take all the abuse in the world than to see her little sister go through it.

I'm afraid something bad will happen to my abuser.

Cassie's stepdad told her that if she ever told, he would kill himself. She loved him and would never want him to do something that horrible, even if it meant that her abuse would stop.

The feelings of a child trapped in an abusive relationship are usually very conflicted. If the person who abused you was someone you knew, loved, and trusted, you probably feel as if you're riding an emotional roller coaster. Life might seem like a fantasy world, where things aren't exactly real and every feeling is unexpected and surprising. One minute, you may hate your abuser for the pain he has caused you; the next, you may love him because of what he has meant to you at times in your life.

You may think that telling would betray the person who abused you because you still feel love for him despite the wrong he has done. I understand your feelings. My stepfather did terrible things to me. He manipulated and controlled me and caused me great fear and uneasiness. But he was also my stepfather, the husband of my mother, and the father of my best friend. He was an important father figure in my life, and I loved him. I didn't want him to be in trouble; so throughout my childhood, I made mental excuses for him. I've heard many of you make the same kinds of excuses:

"He was just DEPRESSED."

"He was DRUNK when it happened."

"He was going through A HARD TIME."

"HE DIDN'T KNOW it was wrong."

"He said HE WAS SORRY."

Please know that excuses like these are rationalizations. They are your mind's attempt to resolve your confusion by making your abuser's behavior seem rational. They may sound like plausible reasons for his behavior, but the fact is they are lies that keep you from acting on what you know to be true by keeping you in denial.

Denial is a defense mechanism that helps us survive traumas like sexual abuse. Even after a decade of abuse, I denied it. To my mind, there was no way I could have been abused. I didn't think something like that could happen in a family like mine. And I just couldn't accept that my stepdad would do something bad to me. I decided that *my* situation had to be unique. I shoved the thoughts out of mind as soon as they came. I was in denial.

I'm afraid of what everybody will think.

Survivors are often terrified of what others think about them. A year after I told my secret and began a new life free of sexual abuse, none of my friends—not even my best friend—knew about my past. I was still so ashamed, and I thought everyone would think it was my fault and wouldn't like me anymore.

Whenever kids at school would ask me about it, I would deny it to their faces and sometimes run to the bathroom to cry. It was the worst feeling in the world. I thought people were looking at me and labeling me. *Molested by her stepdad. Gross.* This is a common concern for many survivors of abuse. We're afraid others will believe the same things about us that we believe about ourselves.

THERE'S NO WAY ANYONE CAN KNOW JUST BY LOOKING AT YOU THAT YOU'VE BEEN SEXUALLY ABUSED.

If our pain is very deep, we may believe that others can immediately identify us as victims of sexual abuse. We're afraid it's obvious to everyone. This fear seems ridiculous to those who have never been sexually abused, but for those who have, it can be very real. This is another fear based on a lie. There's no way anyone can know just by looking at you that you've been sexually abused.

Fears based on lies are powerful deterrents to telling others that we've been abused. If it weren't so difficult to tell, I wouldn't have a full-time career devoted to helping abuse survivors find their voice. I wouldn't meet thousands of students who are still carrying around the pain of their dark secret. I wouldn't be traveling all over the country with this message of hope and healing.

Recently I met a friend for lunch at a Chinese bistro. After paying the tab, we opened our fortune cookies. Mine said something like "That was not *chicken*." (Actually, I don't remember what it said, but that's what I was thinking at the time!) My friend's fortune cookie said something far more profound: "Fear is interest paid on a debt you may not owe." I had to think about that statement for a while and really let it sink in. You should too.

The lie that your abuse was your fault keeps you in bondage and afraid to tell. It's the soil in which many other lies about yourself take root and grow. On my own healing journey, I suffered from the same false belief Anna did. Even after I told my secret, I struggled to believe that the abuse wasn't my fault.

My shame was overwhelming, and to be free to heal, I needed to go back to when sexual abuse first planted this lie in my soul and to allow others to help me replace it with the truth.

"DON'T BE AFRAID! SPEAK OUT! DON'T BE SILENT!"
"DON'T BE AFRAID! SPEAK OUT! DON'T BE SILENT!"

"DON'T BE AFRAID! SPEAK OUT! DON'T BE SILENT!"

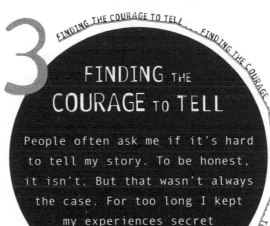

3

FINDING THE COURAGE TO TELL

People often ask me if it's hard to tell my story. To be honest, it isn't. But that wasn't always the case. For too long I kept my experiences secret because of who I

——→

"DON'T BE

AFRAID!

SPEAK OUT!

DON'T BE SILENT!"

Acts 18:9

thought I was. In my mind, I was a normal Christian girl with a lot going for me. I feared that if I told my secret, I would lose all of that.

Silence delays the healing process by perpetuating the hurt, shame, and guilt of adult survivors. It imprisons us in a dark closet built on falsehood and papered with lies. It also protects sexual offenders by allowing them to continue to abuse their victims. It's never too early or too late to tell.

Easier said than done, right? If you're a survivor of sexual abuse, telling someone may well be the one thing you fear most in your life. I know how you feel, and so do thousands of others. Nevertheless, you must find the courage to tell, for breaking the silence is the first major step in moving from silence to healing.

BREAKING THE SILENCE

I always wanted to tell my mother that my stepdad was abusing me, but for a decade my fears kept me silent. Then in the summer of 1994, when I was fourteen years old, something happened that changed my life forever.

The weekend began like any other. It was Friday afternoon. My mom and I were driving into town to pick up Steph to spend the weekend with us. As she was driving, Mom told me that she wanted to go back to college to become a math teacher. But when she had talked with Vince about it, he had become very angry with her. They were sitting outside on the deck when she shared her dreams with him. When she finished talking, he walked into the house and began yelling, swearing, and throwing things across the room. When he came back outside, he verbally attacked her. She told me she had felt very afraid of him.

Then Mom asked me if Vince had ever done anything bizarre around me.

I couldn't look her in the eyes, so I just nodded my head. She asked me what he had done. I was quiet. I pretended to listen to the radio, but I was really imagining what she would say if I told her my secret. It had been my reality for so long that I wasn't even sure it was wrong. Vince had always told me it was normal. I was also afraid Mom would think it was my fault, just as I did. But I knew that if I was ever going to tell her, this was the time. She had given me the opportunity, and it was now or never.

Mom's eyes looked very concerned, yet loving. I trusted my mother, and that gave me the courage to tell her the secret my stepfather had made me promise never to tell.

FOR THE FIRST TIME IN MY LIFE, I KNEW THAT WHAT MY STEPFATHER HAD DONE WAS WRONG.

Mom slammed on the brakes and pulled our minivan to the side of the road. For the first time in my life, I *knew* that what my stepfather had done was wrong. Suddenly, the memories came flooding back. I told Mom everything I could remember, and she got very quiet. She hugged me, and I could tell that she was doing her best not to cry. She told me that she didn't know what we were going to do but not to worry. She would take care of it.

We left home the following Monday. That night, in the attic of my grandmother's house, my mom and I prayed and believed together that, however things turned out, it would be the best for everyone involved. She reported the abuse to our local children's services, and they interviewed each of us. The next day, a police detective called to tell us that they had called my stepfather in for questioning and that he had denied everything. We were scheduled to go to court in a month, the first day of my freshman year of high school.

The days that followed were the most frightening days of our lives. We believed that if Vince found us, he would kill us. We went from house to house, staying with various friends and family, trying to hide from him. The phone seemed to ring off the hook everywhere we went. Exactly one week after we left our home, the detective called to tell my mother that two policemen were on their way to talk with us. When they arrived, they informed us that my stepfather had committed suicide.

We could never have predicted that breaking the silence would have such a tragic and traumatic aftermath. I was both relieved and furious. I wouldn't face any more abuse, but Vince would never have to admit to what he had done, and I hated him for that. I knew that life would be an uphill battle as my mother and I faced family, friends, and an unknown future.

My stepfather was in his grave, but his legacy of hush lived on. Though telling my secret brought me some relief, I still felt extremely ashamed. Mom protected me by not revealing my secret to our community. At the funeral, she shouldered the blame, allowing people to believe that Vince had killed himself because she had left him. To escape the stigma associated with this filthy violation, I planned to put it back under lock and key and never tell again. It took me awhile to realize that I had to continue to break the silence if I was ever going to believe that the abuse wasn't my fault.

DECISIONS TO MAKE

As you prepare to break your own silence, you'll have some important decisions to make. You'll need to decide whom you should tell, how much you should tell, and if you should tell the authorities.

Whom should I tell?

When you first tell your secret, the response you receive will influence the route your healing will take in the immediate future. This means you need to be very selective about whom you choose to tell. The person you confide in should be someone you trust—someone you think will believe you, accept you, love you, protect you, and walk with you along the road ahead. Trust will continue to be important as you tell your story to others.

Following my stepfather's death, the courts closed the case by listing the abuse charges as "substantiated." This meant that his suicide proved his guilt. I was immediately scheduled for counseling in an adjoining town. My counselor was an older blue-haired woman. She was very nice, but she wasn't anyone I was interested in confiding in, so I set out to convince her that I was a child prodigy who didn't need counseling.

To my mind, sexual abuse was simply something that had happened to me, something I could handle without missing a beat. I didn't need to talk about my memories because they didn't bother me. I kept this up, and after only a few sessions, she finally agreed with me: I had a bright future, and my secret wasn't going to hold me back.

Despite my denial, I *did* want to talk with someone. It just wasn't going to be someone I didn't even know, much less trust. I thought about my junior high music teacher, Mrs. Bell. (Pretty appropriate name for a music teacher, don't ya think?) She had attended my stepfather's funeral, and it meant a lot to me that she came. She didn't say much to me then, but I felt drawn to her. Although I wasn't sure why, I trusted her.

One day after class, I asked Mrs. Bell if I could speak with her. I told her my story and the truth about my stepfather's death. She gave me the response I wish all survivors would receive when they tell their story. She hugged me and told me that it wasn't my fault, that I didn't deserve it, and that she didn't think any differently about me. In fact, she cared for me even more. For about a year after that, she met with me after school whenever I needed to talk.

I chose to talk to Mrs. Bell because at that time my mom felt a lot of guilt for not having known about the abuse. Even though I talked to her about most of it, there were some things I wasn't ready to tell her because I thought they would just make her feel worse.

Like me, many survivors of sexual abuse have to decide when and how to tell their family. This can be a hard step for those who don't want to hurt their family. Jamie, a college sophomore, said, "Something I haven't done is tell my parents about what happened to me. Part of me thinks it will just make them worry more." Some have never told anyone their secret, and they want to tell their parents first. Others have already shared their story with friends or counselors, and now they want to tell their family.

It's always your choice whether or not to tell. However, I think that if at any point you feel a burden to tell your family, you should do it. Keeping a secret from your parents or siblings can end up hurting them more by building an invisible wall between you.

Shawnna's cousin raped her when she was thirteen, but she didn't tell her family until several years later. Looking back, she saw how keeping her secret had caused her relationship with her family to start to fall apart. Shawnna had wanted to protect her parents and brother from the knowledge that she had been hurt, but in trying to keep her abuse secret, she began to withdraw from them. She feared that if she allowed them to get too close, they would suspect the truth or she would inadvertently reveal it. She began lying about inconsequential things totally unrelated to the rape.

After hearing me speak, Shawnna called a family meeting at which she told them the truth and asked them to forgive her. They responded lovingly and wiped the slate clean. Their relationship has been renewed, and now they talk about everything. Shawnna says she just wishes she had told them earlier.

Women often ask me if it's safe to tell a man. I think it depends on why you choose him as the one to confide in. Your reason for choosing a particular confidant must be that you consider that person someone you can trust to be there for you, listen to you, and tell you that it wasn't your fault. This may or may not be a man, but it shouldn't be someone you're romantically interested in.

It's vital that you don't allow intimate confiding to turn into something more. This can throw so many loops and weird dynamics into the healing process that it could be very harmful to you for years to come. You both must often depends on <u>whom</u> you tell.

recognize that your relationship is based on friendship, and you both must have the character and discipline to not allow it to be anything more than that.

How much should i tell?

This is up to you. It will be different for each person, and it may change as you heal and grow. Telling is a process.

How *much* you tell often depends on *whom* you tell. If you're telling someone who doesn't need to know everything, it would be better to keep your explanation general. The details are important only for your healing process, not for the listener. If you're telling a counselor or someone else who is helping with your healing, I would encourage you to give the details.

Sharing the details of my abuse with Mrs. Bell started slowly. The first time we met, we both sat facing the same direction so I didn't have to look her in the face. She asked me to tell her what I remembered and how I was feeling. It was very difficult to put into words what I saw playing over and over in my head, but I remember telling her about one of the few clear memories I had at that point. I was crying and feeling very shivery and scared. She kept repeating that I would be okay, that she cared about me, and that it wasn't my fault. I told her what I could see and feel and hear and smell.

Mrs. Bell told me that it would help me to really say it, to say everything, to tell the worst parts, and to use the right words for them. I hated that. I didn't want to say any "dirty" words; I just wanted to get each story out as fast as I could. But as we continued to meet and my trust in her grew, I saw that doing what she suggested was helping, for my burden was being lifted.

While I was telling her what I remembered, it felt as if I had a really heavy blanket on my head and shoulders; but afterward, the blanket didn't seem as heavy as before. As we continued to talk after school, every time I shared more details, I felt the blanket on me getting lighter. My burden was being lifted bit by bit, story by story. Once I told a memory, it was as if I didn't own it anymore.

Should I tell the authorities?

I'm so thankful for my mother's response when I told her my secret. She believed me and took steps to protect me at all costs. However, I know from the thousands of stories I've heard that my mother's response wasn't typical.

When fifteen-year-old Marcie told her mother that her grandfather had abused her, her mother slapped her face. Everyone in her family knew about the abuse, but they all told her to keep quiet. *Hush!* Their reaction sent Marcie the message that she wasn't worth protecting.

> ONCE I TOLD A MEMORY, IT WAS AS IF I DIDN'T OWN IT ANYMORE.

When Hector told his parents that his uncle was sexually abusing him, they didn't respond at all. They showed no emotion and didn't say anything. Life went on as usual, as if nothing had happened.

Melanie said, "I always wanted to tell, but I have an older cousin who told all of us that she had been abused, and my family pretended like it didn't happen and didn't matter. Why should I think my situation is any different?"

If you're one of many brave survivors who once found the courage to tell but weren't believed, I want you to know that I admire your courage. You're a strong survivor, and I'm very proud of you for opening up despite your fear.

As difficult as this may sound, I want to encourage you to try again. If the first person you tell doesn't believe you, tell someone else! Don't give up until you find someone who will believe you and protect you. If your nonabusing parent doesn't help you, tell another family member you think you can trust or your best friend's parents or a teacher, principal, counselor, nurse, or pastor. If none of them do the right thing, go to someone who *must* do what is right. I encourage you to report your abuse with the intent to prosecute for three reasons.

First, it will help stop more abuse from occurring. Studies show that nearly 70 percent of child sex offenders have between one and nine victims and that at least 20 percent have from ten to forty victims. An average serial child molester can have as many as four hundred victims in his lifetime. Stopping your abuser will keep lots of other kids from suffering the pain of abuse.

Second, it might force your abuser to get treatment. Although there are no guarantees that your abuser will become a better person, at least with treatment there's a chance that he will no longer abuse others.

Third, it's one of the only ways that you yourself can bring justice to the situation. Knowing you had the courage to do what's right and perhaps save another innocent victim from abuse will move you ahead on your healing journey.

It's scary to think about being all alone in your fight for what's right in the event that your family chooses sides, and it's frightening to think about facing your abuser in court. This is a decision only you can make. Sometimes reporting will actually make things worse for a time. It got worse for my mother and me before it got better. But it did get better —way better!

WHAT TELLING WILL DO

As an abused child, you were told over and over in many ways to keep this secret. As an adult survivor, your mind may still be telling you to hush. You may still be afraid to open up. I understand that. But I also understand a couple of other things that can help you overcome your fear. First, I understand that courage isn't the absence of fear; it's the willingness to act in the face of fear. It's what enables you to tell your story despite your fear. I also understand what telling your secret will do for your healing:

It will help VALIDATE your experience and feelings.

It will help you understand YOUR INNOCENCE and your abuser's guilt.

It will HELP you realize that you're NOT ALONE.

It will help you OPEN UP TO OTHERS so they can comfort and encourage you.

It will help you experience HEALTHY EMOTIONS and honest relationships.

It will help restore your TRUST.

It will help B O O S T your self-esteem.

It will help affirm your SELF-WORTH.

It will help you be a source of COMFORT to others.

No matter how complicated my life got after I told my secret, I knew that it had been the right thing to do. Telling released me from my past so I could embrace the future. The more I told, the more it helped free me from the pain and shame.

When you get right down to it, this isn't your secret to keep. It's the secret of the one who hurt you. He's the one who was wrong. She's the one who was to blame. The person who chose to violate you is the one who should be concerned with keeping this secret, not you.

I want to encourage you to not wait for others to break the silence, because most likely, they never will. You yourself need to speak up, not only to break free from your own bondage, but also to help someone else find the courage to do the same.

For years I believed that I was alone and that no one else could relate to what I had gone through. No one ever told me how many other kids were going through the same thing. Even if they had, I might not have believed them because I'd never heard anyone talk about being sexually abused. I had no idea that other victims needed someone to speak up. They needed *me* to speak up!

I want you to know that if you have been sexually abused in any way, *you are not alone!* As I travel and speak, I meet so many young people who are silently hurting and desperately in need of healing. When does their healing begin? For many of them, it begins when I share my story. It could begin for someone *you* know when you share *your* story. Your courage could spark his or her healing as well.

If not you, who?

If not now, when?

Don't submit to the bondage of silence. Break it! Tell your story over and over. Write it down and read it over and over. The more you speak it and the more you write it, the less power it will have over you. Cry and yell if you have to. Get it all out! Do what works best for you, but do it until the silence is broken. If you don't find the courage to tell, your fears can lead you to cope in unhealthy ways that will just perpetuate the bondage you feel.

DON'T SUBMIT TO THE BONDAGE OF SILENCE.

BREAK IT!

"NOT BY MIGHT NOR BY POWER, BUT BY MY SPIRIT," SAYS THE Lord ALMIGHTY.
"NOT BY MIGHT NOR BY POWER, BUT BY MY SPIRIT," SAYS THE Lord ALMIGHTY.

"NOT BY MIGHT NOR BY POWER, BUT BY MY SPIRIT," SAYS THE Lord ALMIGHTY.

4

IN SEARCH
OF POWER

Heidi was abused by just about
everybody in her family—her
father, her mother, her two
brothers, and her grandfather.
"I don't think there are any
good people out there,"
she says.

"NOT BY

MIGHT NOR BY

POWER, BUT

BY MY SPIRIT,'"

SAYS THE LORD ALMIGHTY.

Zechariah 4:6 NIV

It's about power and control.

"Everyone is bad. I will never trust anyone, because if I do, they will just end up hurting me." Heidi tried to protect herself by shutting everyone out, and as a result, she became a depressed, nervous, mistrusting hermit.

As survivors of sexual abuse, our actions and attitudes are deeply rooted in our past. We learned at an early age that when someone else was in control, we could get hurt. Many survivors tell me that if they had been in control, they wouldn't have been abused. They think that their inability to escape abuse was due to their powerlessness.

Sexual abuse isn't about sex. It's about power and control. As our abusers once used their power to control us, now we use our power to control our life. Coping mechanisms are a way for us to turn the tables. As we cope with the pain of our past, we quickly realize that we have the power to disguise ourselves, to damage ourselves, and even to destroy ourselves.

OUR POWER TO DISGUISE

When we feel weak and vulnerable, it's normal to fall back on our natural strengths. This is the way I chose to cope with my abuse. My behavior may not have seemed extreme, but it nevertheless prevented me from being the real me and made it difficult for me to maintain healthy relationships.

In my search for power, I became a control freak, a people pleaser, a perfectionist, a tough girl, and a princess in a tower. Do you see yourself in any of these categories? If so, realize that they are masks that prevent you from getting to the root of your pain.

The control freak

The desire for power is often a subconscious defense mechanism. At the time, I didn't recognize my need for control. But as I look back at some of my actions and relationships, I realize that I was wounded and needed to feel safe. As a result, I was a controlling individual. In high school and college, I believed I had to be in charge at all times to keep from being hurt.

This carried over into my relationships with guys. I looked for boyfriends I could change. Control seems especially necessary when we don't know whom we can trust. To my mind, finding a guy I could shape into the kind of person I could trust would keep me safe. In one particular relationship, I was not only controlling, but also extremely mistrusting. I seemed to always be looking for evidence that he was going to leave me. I needed to know where he was at all times and what he was doing. If he didn't call when he said he would, my mind would blow the situation way out of proportion.

Little things like this can seem huge when we've been abused. Our mind seems to automatically focus on the negative. We believe things like "men can't be trusted" and "others will always leave me," and we look for any evidence that supports these false beliefs.

The perfectionist

Survivors of abuse also tend to believe that the love they receive depends on their performance. I pushed myself to be involved in every activity I could. I not only had to participate, but I also had to be the leader. It wasn't acceptable not to be elected president or captain of every group I was in. Getting the highest awards and the best grades made me feel that I was in control of my life and of those around me. If I was in control, I didn't have to trust anyone.

I also coped by filling my plate with as many clubs, sports, and studies as possible. I was so involved with extracurricular activities and so intent on getting good grades that I didn't have time to think about my problems. I believed that this gave me control over my life by keeping out bad thoughts and memories.

The tough girl

Toni is a very bright college student. She's at the top of her class and extremely focused. She's also very bossy and aggressive, always ready to argue. Toni often brags that she hasn't cried once in five years. Her tough shell seems real to many who pass her every day on campus, but the day I met her in a one-on-one session in the chaplain's office, I saw right through that mask to the lonely, sad, hurting girl inside. This wasn't difficult for me because I had already seen it in many other "tough girls," including myself.

> I THOUGHT THAT THE POWER TO CONTROL MY EMOTIONS MEANT THAT NOBODY COULD HURT ME AGAIN.

In high school and college I prided myself on not having cried for a long time. I would never cry in front of others. It sounds silly now, but at the time I thought that if I cried, it would reveal my weaknesses. I wouldn't even cry at a movie because

I didn't want to ruin the tough-girl image I was trying to project. Sometimes I would go to the movie theater to see tearjerkers just to prove I could watch without crying. I had a perfect record going of not crying at sad movies—though I came pretty close when Bambi's mom died!

I thought that the power to control my emotions meant that nobody could hurt me again. I believed that if I created a tough outer shell, no one could use my weaknesses against me because, as far as I was concerned, they could never get close enough to find any.

The people pleaser

Children who are victims of sexual abuse learn that in order for people to love them, they must please others by doing what they ask. Once established, this core belief carries over into their adult behavior. They believe that pleasing others at all times has the power to keep them safe.

Lisa's desire to please took her from being an outgoing leader in childhood to being a frightened follower as a teenager. She wanted her peers to like her, so she did what they told her to do, even if it meant shoplifting at the local gas station or getting high. She dressed the way her friends dressed and talked the way they talked. She told me that she didn't feel like herself with them, but they accepted her and she didn't want to lose that.

I had a hard time saying no to people. When I was asked to head up a new project at school or lead a new outreach at church, I always said yes, even though I knew I didn't have time for it. I wanted everyone to be happy with me, so I always did what anyone asked.

In other cases, survivors make themselves doormats in order to please others. They never offer an opinion and never say or do anything that could make waves. They are submissive and often extremely apologetic, taking the blame for everything, even when others are clearly at fault. They may also seem very whiny or babyish. Shedding tears or saying sorry all the time can be a manipulative way of asserting power over others.

The princess in a tower

Building protective walls around ourselves is another way we try to gain power.

Like the princess Rapunzel, I thought I could sit safely in my castle high above the ground with the bridge over the moat drawn up. I knew that letting down my guard could be disastrous, and I couldn't take that risk. I assumed that if you couldn't get near me, you couldn't hurt me. So I used my smarts to pick out the best blocks of stone and my strength to build enormous walls all by myself. I didn't need any help, and I didn't want any visitors.

Walls take many forms. I've met some beautiful young women who make themselves as unattractive as possible to keep people away. They refuse to bathe, wear makeup, or brush their teeth. Some overeat in an attempt to literally hide in their skin; others wear very baggy clothing or cut off all their hair.

Please understand that these behaviors won't protect you from abuse. You weren't abused because you were attractive or sexy or thin or irresistible. It had nothing to do with you. It was nothing you did, wore, or said. It wasn't your fault. The abuse happened because there was something wrong with your abuser. It was his problem, and he was to blame. Nothing you do to your body now will change that.

OUR POWER TO DAMAGE

As adults, survivors of childhood sexual abuse often carry around a lot of hidden shame. Our shame is rooted in the lies we believe about ourselves, especially the lie that the abuse was somehow our fault. This false belief causes us to not only feel rejected by others, but also to reject ourselves, even to the point of self-hatred. This can lead to abnormal behaviors like eating disorders and self-injury.

One of the easiest ways to get power over our bodies is to control our food intake. This is why some abuse survivors develop eating disorders. Some starve their bodies (anorexia nervosa) and some binge and purge their food as a daily ritual (bulimia). Others rely on a combination of these disorders to cope. An obsession with thinness is often a cover-up for their preoccupation with their inner pain. Their eating disorder is their attempt to protect themselves by controlling the things they believe led to their abuse or to purge the pain they feel within.

"When I was young, my father would take me out on dates and buy me expensive food and gifts," Andrea told me. "These weren't your normal father/daughter dates, although I thought they were at the time. I was 'Daddy's little woman,' as he would say. He would take out my mother's lingerie and make me put it on to show him. He would always say that I looked better in it than Mommy because she was too thin.

"When I turned thirteen, I gained a lot of weight, and my father liked it. I had already decided that I never wanted to look attractive to him, and now I decided that all the pain would go away if I weighed less. So I began to throw up after I ate.

"Sadly, as I continued playing the game with my body, I ended up losing. It messed up parts of my life that I never thought it would affect. And now it's a part of me that I can't get rid of. It is a part of me that I hate."

When people cause intentional harm or pain to their own body as a way of coping, it's called self-harm, self-abuse, self-mutilation, or self-injury. A common form of self-injury today is "cutting." All over the country, I meet abuse victims who are harming their own bodies by cutting themselves. Many people think it's just a fad, but for survivors it's much more than that. They don't do it with their friends to be cool; they do it in secret to kill their inner pain. The underlying attitude is: "If I'm going to be hurt, *I'll* be the one who inflicts the pain."

To tell the truth, I'm hesitant to talk about cutting. When I asked a friend of mine how she first came up with the idea to cut herself, she said that she read about it in a magazine. Her statement devastated me. I believe that telling the truth about real-life issues is the way to freedom, but obviously the truth can sometimes get twisted. In bringing this terrible problem into the light, my prayer is that facing it will set captives free. You don't need physical wounds to match the ones you feel inside!

As children, abuse survivors weren't allowed to tell. Later as adults, they don't know how. They're afraid of what might come out. Their lips are sealed, so they try to speak with their body. Cutters often tell me that no one understands how they feel. For Ty, a razor blade took the place of an understanding friend. When the tension of pent-up emotions became unbearable, cutting was how he tried to find relief.

I hurt for those of you who feel misunderstood. I realize that you can't put what you feel into words. Nevertheless, hurting yourself won't give you more control over your life.

"Cutting just masks the problem for a little while," Kylene says. "It's still there after the cut heals. Then I'm left with an ugly scar and the same feeling I had inside before I hurt myself. When I think about it now, it all seems so stupid."

If you've chosen to deal with your pain through an eating disorder or self-injury, I want you to know that I understand. I know that you're doing what you think you need to do to get through the pain and shame. But the problem is that exercising this kind of power over your body just perpetuates the abuse you're trying to escape. This kind of coping won't ever heal your inner wound. It will only lead to more wounds that will require their own healing.

In my opinion, you'll never stop relying on unhealthy coping mechanisms until you dig deep into the pain in your past. Talking to a counselor or someone you trust can help you work through the hurt that remains. Once your past is healed, the unhealthy coping mechanism will shed itself like old skin.

OUR POWER TO DESTROY

Some survivors of abuse try to take their own lives. They see suicide as a way to end the torment by exercising the power they have over their own bodies.

Life is hard, and working through issues of abuse is even harder. Just making it through today might be a great accomplishment for you. If you've ever contemplated suicide, I want you to know that you're not alone. There were times when I envisioned my funeral. I didn't exactly want to die, but I did want my pain to end. I know many others who fantasize about how and when they will end it all.

A friend of mine once wrote a letter to an abuse victim who was contemplating suicide. In case you're thinking about ending your life, I want to share parts of it with you. Appropriately, my friend's name is Hope.

"I was severely abused as a child. When I was nineteen, I felt as you may feel now. The pain was intense, and there was no guarantee that it would ever be any different. It seemed pointless to go on if this was all life had to offer.

I DIDN'T EXACTLY WANT TO DIE, BUT I DID WANT MY PAIN TO END.

"There came a day when I knew for certain that I would kill myself. I planned it all out, and I knew I was going to go through with it. I bought a bottle of pills, got in my car, and headed for a secluded place in the woods. I knew no one would find me in time to save me.

"On my way I stopped at a red light. As I sat there, I felt an overwhelming need to decide between turning right or left. Turning right would lead me to the woods and be the end of me. Turning left would lead me . . . where? I had no way of knowing. I only knew that it would mean hanging on a little while longer. Everything in me wanted to turn right, but in my head I heard over and over 'turn left, turn left.' I can still feel the fear that overtook me. I knew I wasn't playing around. This was it. If I turned right, there would be no more Hope.

"When the light changed, I felt my hands turn the wheel left almost in spite of myself. Somewhere deep inside, the survivor in me was willing to give life a little more time.

"When I turned left instead of right that night, I didn't know that peace and joy and love and laughter lay down the road. I didn't know that I would fall in love with and marry a wonderful man and have three incredible daughters. No, I didn't know all that; and if someone had told me, I wouldn't have believed it. I had no use for men. I thought all they did was hurt and abuse. I would have told anyone that I would never allow myself to be vulnerable enough to love a man, let alone marry him.

"My friend, you have been on the earth only a fraction of the time you are meant to be here. There's so much ahead of you that you just can't see or even begin to imagine. You don't have to know how it's all going to turn out. You only have to decide, 'Can I do this for another minute . . . keep breathing for another hour? Can I try for just one more afternoon and then one more night? Will it be worth the risk to try, even for just another hour?' Only you can decide if it's worth trying for one more moment."

If you often think about committing suicide, I urge you to contact someone who will listen and can help. Contact a counseling service, a suicide hotline, or your local child or family services. With intervention, life can get better. Suicide is never the answer!

NOT in OUR POWER

As I look back, I see that none of the ways I chose to cope with abuse made me feel any less vulnerable. I wasn't in control. I still didn't trust others, and I was still afraid of being hurt again. As it is for many survivors of childhood trauma, my need for power and control was a mask covering up my inner fear. What came naturally to me didn't necessarily reflect the real me.

My means of coping were also exhausting me. I kept it up for a while, but once I was in college I realized that trying to stay in control only magnified my fears. The actions and attitudes I thought would keep me safe had actually imprisoned me in a dark closet of my own making. And all the things I was trying to escape—bad memories, shame, guilt, pain—were right in there with me.

Many of us don't know why we act the way we do! That's the reason I studied psychology in college. I wanted to know why I was holding things back and afraid to be the real me. I had an inkling that my actions and attitudes stemmed from my past, but I wanted to know for sure.

That's when I decided to see a counselor. Although telling Mrs. Bell the details of my abuse had helped bring healing to my spirit, I had continued to stuff my feelings throughout high school. Women, especially teachers and ladies in my church, often commented on how sweet and kind I was, but to my peers at school I seemed more like a tough tomboy. The real Nicole wasn't always who she appeared to be on the outside. The real Nicole was a compassionate, sensitive, sometimes emotional girl who wanted to share her heart with the world.

In my desire to be free, I went to the college counseling center. On the way, my pride raised its ugly head. *People like me don't go to counselors!* I told myself. *I'm a college athlete . . . and a psychology major, for crying out loud!* I didn't want anyone to know I was seeing a counselor. I'm embarrassed to admit this, but as I slipped through the door, I pulled my hooded basketball sweatshirt over my head and crossed my arms over the number twenty-two on the front.

What a breakthrough it was for me to get that far!

Although you may also find it difficult to seek out a counselor, finding one who will listen to you, keep your conversations confidential, and support you will facilitate your healing journey. On your own, you may have a difficult time identifying the triggers that cause you to do what you do, and a wise counselor can help.

Counseling was great for me. I went for an hour every Wednesday afternoon for my entire sophomore year. My counselor and I talked about abuse, anger, family, trust, relationships, perfectionism, and all kinds of stuff that helped me see why I was the way I was. She listened and helped me grow and heal.

I REALIZED THAT TRYING TO STAY IN CONTROL ONLY MAGNIFIED MY FEARS.

By the end of the year, I had broken out of my tough-girl shell, climbed down from my lofty tower, and started crying during sad movies—even when some of my teammates were in the room! I didn't try to squelch my feelings anymore. I allowed myself to experience joy and happiness, as well as sadness and loss. That was liberating for me. I was learning that it was a lie that being vulnerable would cause me to get hurt. My relationships were becoming so much more real and meaningful. I felt so alive!

Choosing to exercise our power to disguise, damage, or destroy ourselves results in a variety of coping mechanisms. Some are clearly abnormal and self-destructive; some seem natural and even rational. Some, like addiction to drugs, alcohol, or sex, aren't really ways to cope with the pain; they are ways to escape it. Yet all have one thing in common: They are all unhealthy ways of coping that keep us bound in the prison of our past.

Do you feel powerless today? Are you struggling with the painful residue of childhood sexual abuse? The solution doesn't lie in your power to control your body, your environment, or others. And as much help as counselors can be, it isn't in their power to heal you. For that, you need a greater power, one that comes only as you seek a personal relationship with the Almighty Healer, God.

"YOU WILL KNOW THE TRUTH, AND THE TRUTH WILL SET YOU FREE."
"YOU WILL KNOW THE TRUTH, AND THE TRUTH WILL SET YOU FREE."

"YOU WILL KNOW THE TRUTH, AND THE TRUTH WILL SET YOU FREE."

5

THE TRUTH THAT SETS YOU FREE... THAT SETS YOU FREE FREE FREE FREE

THE
TRUTH THAT
SETS YOU FREE

When Rachel was a child, her foster family sexually abused her. They told her that the only thing she was good for was to keep Dad happy. On a daily →

"YOU WILL

KNOW THE

TRUTH, AND

THE TRUTH WILL

SET YOU FREE."

John 8:32

basis they told her that she didn't deserve to be loved and that no one wanted her, not even God. She grew up with these lies embedded in her mind and heart. As an adult, she couldn't receive love because she believed that she was too worthless to be loved by anyone, especially God.

I've already talked about some of the lies abuse survivors believe about themselves in order to help you understand why you might be afraid to break the silence. When we find the courage to tell, we take the first major step on our healing journey. When we embrace the truth that the abuse wasn't our fault, we take the second. But there are other lies that can cause us more problems and pain along the way. Chief among them are the lies we believe about God. Replacing these lies with truth is crucial for healing; for what we believe about God is the source of everything we believe about ourselves, others, and the world.

GETTING TO KNOW GOD

I understand that bringing God into the healing equation may be uncomfortable for some of you. In fact, just thinking about God may stir up a lot of emotions deep inside. You may feel very angry with Him. Or you may have read in the Bible about His love for you, yet really struggle to believe that it applies to you. You may doubt that it's true at all. You may have many questions for which no one can give you a good answer, including me—questions like, *If God loves me, why did this happen*? I want you to know that I understand that. I've been where you are, and I want you to know that your anger, doubts, and questions are normal.

That said, I also believe that you'll never find genuine healing outside of a relationship with God. I would be doing you an injustice to tell you that breaking the silence and accepting the truth about your abuse is the end of your healing. I've heard many speakers say that you should never expect to overcome the pain of sexual abuse. They say that you'll always feel empty inside because of it. My message is different. I just can't leave you there!

You see, I know from my own experience that knowing God was what quieted my questioning heart and allowed His healing waters to flow in and out of my life. Some of you may be thinking, *This may have worked for Nicole because she has a close relationship with God, but it won't work for me. I don't have that.* The greatest news in the world is that you can have one too! What God has done for me, He is longing to do for you.

If we're truthful, we have to admit that our own efforts to cope with our abuse haven't really worked. In many cases, they have just added more problems and injuries; and in the end we still feel shame, pain, and sadness. We've hurt others and ourselves, and in so doing, we've hurt God. But the good news is that all of this can be forgiven and the slate wiped clean. This happens through a personal relationship with God's Son, Jesus Christ, who died on the cross for us so that our sins could be forgiven and we could become children of God.

All you have to do to join God's family is to admit that you've failed Him, realize that you need Him, and ask Him to forgive you and to come into your heart to be your Lord and Savior. This is the simple path to an up-close-and-personal, day-in-and-day-out relationship with the God of the universe.

You'll never find genuine healing outside of a relationship with God.

Once you're in God's family, you can start to get to know Him. Ask Him to show you His true character and reveal to you any lies you've believed about Him. If you long to have Him reveal Himself to you, He will. He wants to show you! No matter what you're struggling with, take it to the Lord. If it's a lack of faith or a lack of desire to know Him more, tell Him. He can handle it. He wants to hear from you. He wants to answer you. He wants to help you.

God will personalize His relationship with you according to who you are and what you need. He sent His Son not only to make forgiveness possible, but also to dry your tears, heal your pain, and give you life in abundance. I know this may be difficult for some of you to believe, but you don't have to take my word for it. God Himself will prove it to you once you have a personal relationship with Him.

If you're ready for a personal relationship with God, you can begin by praying something like this:

Lord, what Nicole has said makes sense to me. I understand that only You can forgive me and free me to heal and truly live. I don't want to go through this healing journey alone; I want to go through it with You. Right now, I accept You as the Lord of my life. Be real to me today. Reveal the lies that have kept me in bondage, and show me how to root them out with the truth in Your Word. Help me live out that truth in my daily life. In Jesus Christ's name I pray. Amen.

Amen means "Yes, it's so," but it also means "Now let's go!" Let's pinpoint the source of the common lies survivors believe about God and then replace them with the truth that will free us to move forward on our healing journey.

REPLACING LIES with TRUTH

Although most lies took root when you were abused as a child, your abuser isn't the only enemy you have. Satan will try to get you with his tricks as well. He doesn't want you to get very far on your healing journey; in fact, he will do everything he can to trip you up by keeping you from knowing the truth. The apostle John says this about him: "He has always hated the truth, because there is no truth in him. When he lies, it is consistent with his character; for he is a liar and the father of lies" (John 8:44).

LISTENING TO SATAN PLANTS THE SEED OF A FALSE BELIEF SYSTEM DEEP WITHIN US.

Listening to Satan plants the seed of a false belief system deep within us.

Dwelling on his lies allows a poisonous vine to grow in the soil of our minds and then spread until it infects every area of our lives. The longer we allow it to live on the inside, the more it will manifest itself on the outside in behavior that keeps us in darkness and bondage. The only way to break free of this oppression is to root out each lie and replace it with truth. When we demolish lies about God, all the lies that stem from a false view of Him will die as well.

Survivors of abuse often find it hard to resist Satan's lies because their own experiences make them seem credible. When you find yourself harboring the Devil's lies in your mind, do what Jesus did when Satan tempted Him in the wilderness: Counter each lie with a truth from God's

Word. This is the way to resist Satan, and God promises that when you do this, "he will flee from you" (James 4:7).

SATAN'S LIE
God abandoned me when I needed Him most.

GOD'S TRUTH:
"God has said, 'I will never fail you. I will never abandon you'" (Hebrews 13:5).

In my experience, this is the number one lie about God that survivors struggle with. I, too, battled it. I spent many nights reading His Word, journaling, and crying out to Him. At last I heard from Him in such a way that I knew without a doubt that He hadn't abandoned me and never would abandon me.

As I grew in my faith and spent time alone with the Lord, I found that He was with me through it all. It may not seem logical (it may even sound crazy), but I've seen the Lord heartbroken for me and for you. I've seen Him crying with us and for us. He cried when I cried. He was angry when I was angry. Sometimes as I closed my eyes and talked to the Lord, I saw Him holding me in His arms and weeping over what had been done to me. God *showed* me that He hadn't abandoned me.

The truth is that the Lord is close to those who are brokenhearted (Psalm 34:18), He will never forget us (Isaiah 49:15), and nothing can separate us from His love (Romans 8:39).

GOD'S TRUTH:

"When you are being tempted, do not say, 'God is tempting me.' God is never tempted to do wrong, and he never tempts anyone else" (James 1:13).

Although most victims of childhood sexual abuse blame themselves for what happened to them, it's also common for them to blame others. Even though the perpetrator is the one who deserves all the blame, it's often too hard for victims to blame an offender who is a parent, caregiver, or someone they love. So others receive the brunt of their anger. This can be the nonoffending parent, a sibling, or even other children at school. Oftentimes, however, it's God.

Adult survivors often blame God as well. Trauma forces us to ask "why" questions: "Why me?" "Why them?" "Why, God?" Left with unanswered questions, we find ourselves either searching for God in a black cloud of doubt, fear, and mistrust, or else running from Him into dark corners, doing our best to deny that He exists.

TRAUMA FORCES US TO ASK "WHY" QUESTIONS: "WHY ME?" "WHY THEM?" "WHY, GOD?"

"Why" questions like these show that sexual abuse is an assault on the very soul of its victims. It causes us to turn against the very One who loves us more than anyone else ever could, our heavenly

Father, Abba God. While I, too, asked all these questions, I eventually came to understand that God wasn't the one responsible for my abuse; my step-father was responsible. The truth is that your abuser chose to hurt you. The abuse wasn't God's doing.

SATAN'S LIE
God is bad, just like my earthly father.

GOD'S TRUTH:

"The Lord is good. His unfailing love continues forever, and his faithfulness continues to each generation" (Psalm 100:5).

The word <u>father</u> can be frightening if your earthly father has abused you. Both teens and adults tell me things like: "I can't accept God as my Father. My real father was a horrible man. I can't trust any father figure." It isn't uncommon for those who have been wounded by an older male, often a father or trusted authority, to feel this way at one time or another.

Don't let Satan deceive you. The truth is that God the Father is, was, and always will be *nothing* like your earthly father. The Bible is quite clear on who God is. Even though I worried about trusting a man again, I knew that God was a whole different ball game. He is nothing like an earthly man. He is more loving, compassionate, merciful, available, trustworthy, and honest than any man you have ever met or ever will meet. He is perfect. He is everything you ever hoped for in a father . . . and then some. Your Abba Father is holier, wiser, and kinder than even your most picture-perfect daddy.

SATAN'S LIE
God doesn't care about child abuse.

GOD'S TRUTH:
" 'If you cause one of these little ones who trusts in me to fall into sin, it would be better for you to have a large millstone tied around your neck and be drowned in the depths of the sea' " (Matthew 18:6).

God has a special place in His heart for children. He loves them and wants them to be treated with love, gentleness, and kindness. He tells us in His Word that it is a very serious offense to lead someone else to sin, especially a child. Any person who harms a child brings God's wrath down upon himself.

God will not stand for child abuse and won't allow it to go unpunished. Child abusers will have to answer to Him. He will see that justice is done. You may not see it happen, and it may not happen the way you want it to, but the Lord will make sure that this sin is paid for.

SATAN'S LIE
God can't heal me.

GOD'S TRUTH:
"By his wounds you are healed" (1 Peter 2:24).

You can be free of the pain of the past—the nightmares, the shame, the fears, the lies. You can nail all of it to the cross. On the cross, Jesus was "beaten so we could be whole. He was whipped so we could be healed" (Isaiah 53:5). If you're a child of God, you don't have to punish your body; Jesus has already taken the beatings for you.

God wants you to know Him personally, and He wants to heal you personally. I feel it burning in my soul that, because we are His children, He aches deeply when we hurt. He wants to take the hurt for us. He doesn't want us to continue to feel the pain. He wants us to give it to Him. And you can. I did. God is now making the effects of sexual abuse disappear from my life. And He will continue to do that as I continue to believe the truth about Him.

YOU DON'T HAVE TO PUNISH YOUR BODY; JESUS HAS ALREADY TAKEN THE BEATINGS FOR YOU.

What lies are you listening to today? Do you believe that God couldn't love you? That He doesn't care about your problems? That He has rejected or forgotten you? Seek the Lord and His Word for the truth.

MAKING THE TRUTH REAL

In the battle for truth, we need to rely on spiritual weapons to defeat our adversary. God has given us all the weapons we need to resist Satan when he attacks. In Ephesians 6:13–18, Paul encourages us to use them:

> Put on every piece of God's armor so you will be able to resist the enemy in the time of evil. Then after the battle you will still be standing firm. Stand your ground, putting on the belt of truth and the body armor of God's righteousness. For shoes, put on the peace that comes from the Good News so that you will be fully prepared. In addition to all of these,

hold up the shield of faith to stop the fiery arrows of the devil. Put on salvation as your helmet, and take the sword of the Spirit, which is the word of God. Pray in the Spirit at all times and on every occasion.

I printed out this passage and taped it on the wall directly in front of my desk, right at eye level. I pray it every morning to prepare myself for whatever fiery darts Satan plans to throw my way that day. This is important for me, and it's important for you too. If we fail to clothe ourselves daily with our spiritual armor, we leave ourselves open to Satan's deception.

You may already be familiar with this passage of Scripture. You might even be able to quote it. But knowing what your spiritual weapons are and actually using them to defeat Satan are two different things. God's truths become real to us only when we put them into practice in our life.

Kim has truly been through hell. She has suffered abandonment, neglect, beatings, rapes, and emotional and verbal abuse. The sins against Kim made her mind an easy target for Satan, who planted his lies there in an effort to destroy her.

"I always felt that I wasn't worth anything to anyone," Kim told me. "Every day I searched Scripture to find out who I was in God's eyes. Then I would go to bed and cry out to the Lord to help me understand what I had read. I *knew* it in my head, but I wanted to *feel* it in my life.

"One night as I was reading and praying, I realized that although I had dealt with a lot of stuff from the past, there were still lies that I believed. So I put on the whole armor of God. I went on a marathon of reading the Scriptures and praying in the Spirit. I asked God to reveal all the lies and replace them with the truth. I wrote out truths on three-by-five index cards and taped them where I would see them every day—on my bathroom mirror, on the door of my refrigerator, on the dashboard of my car.

"I also had a couple of friends who prayed with me over and over again every time I hit bottom. Every time I would cry out to God, He would remind me that He didn't make junk, and that it was a lie of the Enemy for me to believe that I was. He helped me realize that I am a child of the King, a joint heir with Him, and that Satan's lies can never take that away from me. I kept looking to the Lord and relying on His strength to get through the pain. I won the battle of the mind; Satan can't make me believe those lies anymore."

The Lord has given us everything we need to overcome the Devil and his lies. Because He Himself had to do battle with Satan, He knows who and what we're dealing with. I've come to realize that there's no emotion I'll experience in my entire life that Jesus didn't feel while He was on the cross. He has been there . . . and done that! He hurts when we hurt, and He wants to help us, if we will only let Him. "So let us come boldly to the throne of our gracious God. There we will receive his mercy, and we will find grace to help us when we need it most" (Hebrews 4:16).

You may already know some of God's truths in your head. But *feeling* them in your heart and *experiencing* them in your life come when you ask the Lord to show you what they mean and then act on them. He is a personal God. He wants to teach you His truth on a personal level. He wants you to seek Him with your questions so you can find real answers.

LIVING with UNANSWERED QUESTIONS

Even as God's truths and weapons become real In your life, you may still have many unanswered questions about God. To be honest, I still have questions like that—questions such as:

"If God is all-powerful and can beat up the Devil any day He wants, why didn't He stop the abuse when it was happening?"

"Why do bad things happen to good people?"

"Why do we have to go through pain?"

Like King David and Job and many other believers through the centuries, I've wrestled with these questions. I've tossed and turned at night because of them. Even though I still don't have the answers, I'm okay with that now. Why? Because when I invited the God of this universe to come into my world, He came into my life in such a personal and loving way that the questions I still had didn't matter anymore. All that mattered was that I wanted more of Him. I wanted more of His love, His comfort, His peace, and His acceptance. I wanted to be His child, His daughter.

The closer you get to God, the less important your questions will seem. Someday we'll know the answers. Until then, it's okay. For now, God has told us everything we need to know.

People often ask me, "How do I know I'm truly healed in certain areas? I sometimes think it's still there." Remember that when God heals, it's permanent. The big battle is probably won, but you will still have little skirmishes along the way. Satan likes to come into these little scuffles and trick you into thinking they mean more than they do. He wants you to think that God's healing isn't really happening. Don't listen to him! You have to take authority in this situation. At times you just have to say out loud, "Hey! I'm healing. And I'm moving forward in that truth." (Sometimes I throw a "you stupid devil!" in there at the end.)

There are times when your negative thoughts may *not* be from the Enemy. If it's too much of a struggle to stand firm in the Word day after day, you may need more healing. The fight to remain confident in your healing shouldn't consume you. If it does, even though you're doing all you need to stay healthy, it might be a sign that you're now ready to heal an area that hasn't yet been uncovered. Acknowledge the need to receive more healing in that particular area and work through it.

As you replace lies about God with the truth about Him, I encourage you not to go it alone. Lies prevent many survivors from seeing themselves as God sees them, and that keeps them in bondage to fear and self-condemnation. Just as we need someone who can help us break the silence in the beginning, we need someone who can help us see God as He is and ourselves as He sees us.

Do you have someone you trust completely? Someone who knows all about you? If not, you need to find someone like that right away. Seek out a godly mentor or adviser who can help you by guiding and praying for you along your healing journey. When Rachel sought healing from the abuse by her foster parents, her Christian counselor was able to help her break free from the bondage of Satan's lies as he guided her into God's truth.

Moving from silence to healing always means moving *toward* God, the source of light, freedom, and life. It always means moving *away* from Satan, the source of darkness, bondage, and death. One of the greatest gifts God has given you is the power to choose. What you choose to believe about God will eventually determine the choices you make about your healing. If you truly want to be healed, choose to truly believe God. His truth is the truth that sets you free.

I HAVE GIVEN YOU THE CHOICE BETWEEN LIFE AND DEATH....OH, THAT YOU WOULD CHOOSE LIFE SO THAT YOU AND YOUR DESCENDANTS MIGHT LIVE! YOU CAN

MAKE THIS CHOICE BY LOVING THE LORD YOUR GOD, OBEYING HIM, AND COMMITTING YOURSELF FIRMLY TO HIM. THIS IS THE KEY TO YOUR LIFE.

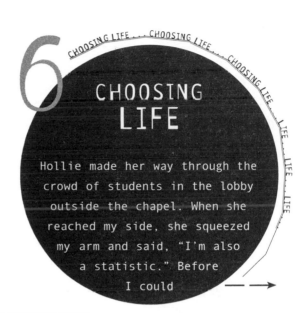

6

CHOOSING LIFE

Hollie made her way through the crowd of students in the lobby outside the chapel. When she reached my side, she squeezed my arm and said, "I'm also a statistic." Before I could

— →

I HAVE GIVEN YOU THE CHOICE BETWEEN LIFE AND DEATH.... OH, THAT YOU WOULD CHOOSE LIFE, SO THAT YOU AND YOUR DESCENDANTS MIGHT LIVE! YOU CAN MAKE THIS CHOICE BY LOVING THE LORD YOUR GOD, OBEYING HIM, AND COMMITTING YOURSELF FIRMLY TO HIM. THIS IS THE KEY TO YOUR LIFE.

Deuteronomy 30:19–20

reply, she said, "I wish I could say I've found healing as you have, but I just don't think it's for me." She told me that her attempts to heal never seemed to work and that she had decided to just suck it up and move on as best she could.

Like Hollie, some of you may be thinking, *God has allowed this, and there's nothing I can do about it.* But I'm here to tell you that this is not God's plan for you! God chooses how, when, and where to heal, and He is the only One who can heal you fully. Nevertheless, I'm a firm believer that you'll heal from sexual abuse only if you choose to be healed. God wants your emotions, your mind, and your will—your soul—to be fully involved in the process. He has given you the power of choice, and He is calling you to make choices about your healing.

CALLED TO EMBRACE THE FUTURE

For seventy years the Israelites suffered in Babylon, held against their will far from the Promised Land. I'm sure they were asking, *Why? Why would God allow the wicked Babylonians to exile and oppress His own people? Why would He allow children to be born into this situation?* It wasn't the children's fault their people were in exile, yet it seemed they had to suffer because of the sins of their fathers.

The exiles couldn't see beyond their suffering, so God had Jeremiah write them a letter to tell them what He had in store for them. The prophet told the Israelites that their captivity was part of God's larger plan to purify and bless them, not to harm them. "'I know the plans I have for you,' says the Lord. 'They are plans for good and not for disaster, to give you a future and a hope'" (Jeremiah 29:11). God was using His people's suffering to draw them to Himself and change their lives for the better. In essence He was saying, "You can trust Me in this situation."

God is saying the same thing to you today: You can trust Him in your situation.

Your past can't be erased, but it isn't your whole story. Your pain isn't the end of you. God can work a miracle in your life. He has something good planned for you, and He can make your life the way you long for it to be. Yes, Satan has robbed you of many things in the past, but God promises to make it all up to you. "I will repay you for the years the locusts have eaten," He says (Joel 2:25 NIV). The Lord has stored up everything the locusts have eaten, and He wants to start giving it all back to you.

GOD IS SAYING THE SAME THING TO YOU TODAY: YOU CAN TRUST HIM IN YOUR SITUATION.

Don't be ashamed because of those stolen years, and don't let the Devil continue to rob you. You can stand tall today. You can live as if you'd never sinned and as if no one had ever sinned against you. You can live as if you were right where you would have been if the Devil hadn't tried to destroy your life. God says, "Fear not; you will no longer live in shame. Don't be afraid; there is no more disgrace for you. You will no longer remember the shame of your youth'" (Isaiah 54:4).

You have a choice. You can embrace the future God has planned for you, or you can cling to the hurts of your past. I pray that you'll choose to put your faith in the One who holds your future in His hands.

CALLED to STEP OUT

Once while Jesus was attending a feast at Jerusalem, He went to the pool of Bethesda. This pool had miraculous healing powers, and many sick people waited there for an angel to stir the waters so they could immerse themselves and be healed. One paralyzed man had been waiting there for thirty-eight years because he didn't have the power to get into the pool by himself. Jesus asked him, "Do you want to get well?" (John 5:6 NIV).

The Lord's question indicates that healing involves an act of the will. Healing begins with a choice, a decision. His command to the man to "Stand up, pick up your mat, and walk!" was a call to action (v. 8). You too have a choice. You can choose to step out on God's healing path, or you can choose to stay in your dark closet of shame and pain.

No one can tell you when you're ready to step out, and no one can tell you that you aren't ready. Only you and the Lord know when it's time. All of us are different, and our reasons for deciding to walk toward the healing waters are as varied as our past and the circumstances of our lives. Many survivors make the life-affirming decision to heal based on an event that opens their eyes to the life they could be leading. Others commit to healing because they've hit rock bottom and have nowhere to go but up. Some want to help others, but they know that their own healing must take place first.

My friend Skye had a verbally abusive father and an emotionally unstable home. In high school and on into college, she cut herself to numb her pain. Then one summer, working with young people brought her to the crossroads of decision about her healing. Many of the kids were also cutters, and they constantly came to her with their stories of hurt. In order to help them, she had to choose to heal from her own pain. She started talking and working through her issues, and that summer she quit cutting. Skye is now living in the freedom of the healing she has already received on her journey, and she continues to reach out to young people in the midst of their hurt.

Why do you play it safe? You're afraid of being hurt again. You're afraid to trust again. It really comes down to this: You have fears, so you hide because it's easy and feels safe. These very real fears provide a great rationale for not stepping out, but they also guarantee that you'll continue to live a life of bondage. If freedom is what you long for, I encourage you to crack open the door of your dark closet and take a look around.

To be free to heal, you must choose to take that first step forward.

CALLED TO PERSEVERE

Whenever you make the decision to step out, realize that healing takes time, commitment, and work. You can't just sit in your counselor's office and hope that the time you log there will do the trick. And you can't expect anyone else to make your healing choices for you. *You* must choose to make healing a priority. You must have goals. You must have an agenda. You must be motivated. You must be active. You must give your healing all the attention it deserves.

Once you step out on God's healing path, I pray that you'll stick it out to the end. The more I travel and the more people I meet, the more I realize that we live in a fallen world in which children are growing up the victims of unhappy, unhealthy adults. Unless they experience healing, these young victims will become the unhappy, unhealthy adults of the next generation. In their hurt, they hurt others, and so the cycle continues. When you persevere in your own healing, you not only help yourself, but you also help others by breaking the cycle of abuse.

WHEN YOU PERSEVERE IN YOUR OWN HEALING, YOU NOT ONLY HELP YOURSELF, BUT YOU ALSO HELP OTHERS BY BREAKING THE CYCLE OF ABUSE.

As the apostle Paul says, "Patient endurance is what you need now, so that you will continue to do God's will. Then you will receive all that he has promised" (Hebrews 10:36). When it gets hard, ask the Lord to strengthen you with His power. I love how *The Message* describes this kind of strength:

> We pray that you'll have the strength to stick it out over the long haul—not the grim strength of gritting your teeth but the glory-strength God gives. It is strength that endures the unendurable and spills over into joy, thanking the Father who makes us strong enough to take part in everything bright and beautiful that he has for us. (Colossians 1:11–12)

Understand that hurt happens; it's inevitable in this life. By accepting this and asking the Lord to be your strength and guide when the going gets rough, you allow His healing waters to flow into those areas where hurt has previously reigned. When you do this, you choose healing over damage control.

CALLED TO BE EMOTIONALLY FREE

"Look!" the risen Savior said to the believers at Laodicia. "I stand at the door and knock. If you hear my voice and open the door, I will come in, and we will share a meal together as friends" (Revelation 3:20).

Offering to share a meal in biblical times had much more spiritual significance than it does in our day. It wasn't like a friend showing up at your door with a pizza to share while you play video games on your big-screen TV. Eating together in Jesus' day meant intimate fellowship, the kind in which you could openly express your feelings, knowing you would be accepted and supported.

This is the kind of relationship God wants to have with you. He wants to come into the deepest part of your being to listen to you, help you, and heal you. That's why He shows up at the door of your heart and knocks. If you've been through the trauma of sexual abuse, you may be so preoccupied with your emotional pain that you can't hear the Lord knocking. If you truly desire healing in your life, you need to release everything your heart has been longing to let out, so the Lord can come in. You have to choose to open the door.

Heather was so deeply wounded in childhood that now she feels hopeless. She has tried to commit suicide several times in the past and now uses an eating disorder to cope with her feelings. Adam was beaten and raped by an older man at a party when he was sixteen. He was full of rage and hated himself for not being able to stop it from happening. Unable to tell anyone what had happened, he began cutting himself. Sidney was sexually abused by her mother's boyfriend between the ages of three and eight. In college, she found alcohol readily available and began to use it to numb her feelings of shame.

It's normal for survivors like Heather, Adam, and Sidney to have trouble expressing their emotions. In order to survive the effects of abuse, they detach themselves from their intense feelings of hopelessness, anger, and shame, often through unhealthy coping mechanisms. But the problem is that you can't be selective in the process; you can't choose to shut yourself off from some feelings and not others. When you detach yourself from the pain and hurt, you cut yourself off from joy and happiness as well.

Keeping your emotions under lock and key keeps you in bondage. When you open the door and allow God to come in and heal you, you'll once again be able to experience a full range of emotions without being afraid of falling apart. You'll begin to experience life fully and completely. Freeing your emotions is part of choosing to truly live.

Where is your freedom? The apostle Paul says it's "wherever the Spirit of the Lord is" (2 Corinthians 3:17). When you hand God the key to your locked-up emotions, you invite His Spirit into your life of pain and confusion and fear. It might sound scary to hand that power over to Him. In fact, it might be the most difficult choice you ever make. But it may also be the most important choice you ever make.

The Lord wants to come in so He can take you back to the day the locusts started wreaking havoc in your life. He wants to help you do the difficult work of remembering and working through your painful emotions. When you invite Him in, His freedom reaches you wherever you are, even as you sit crying inside your dark closet beneath your pile of "stuff" that anyone has yet to see. By sliding out the welcome mat, you allow the healing power of the Spirit to flow freely in your life.

God is knocking at the door of your heart. Won't you ask Him to come in?

CALLED TO BE A MASTERPIECE

One of Michelangelo's greatest masterpieces is his sculpture *David*, which he painstakingly crafted by chipping away at a chunk of flawed marble. As the image of David began to appear, someone asked the artist how he had done it. Michelangelo is said to have replied, "I just took away everything that wasn't David." In Ephesians 2:10, Paul says that we are "God's masterpiecs." Like Michelangelo, God wants to chip away at everything that masks the masterpiece He created us to be.

I HAD TO ALLOW MYSELF TO BE DIFFERENT THAN NORMAL BECAUSE WHAT WAS NORMAL FOR ME BACK THEN WASN'T THE REAL ME.

One of the choices I had to make about my healing was whether or not to allow God to remove my mask and reveal who I was meant to be. As He chipped away at my tough exterior and people-pleasing perfectionism, I had to allow myself to be different than *normal* because what was normal for me back then wasn't the real me. As I travel and speak at high schools and colleges across the nation, I meet many abuse survivors who are wearing masks to hide who they really are.

Veronica is a survivor of abuse who cuts herself. She has accepted that cutting is just a part of who she is and says that "others need to accept that." But engaging in a destructive behavior isn't the same as finding your identity. It's believing a lie about yourself. Although Veronica chose to believe that lie, the truth is that she is wounded and desperately trying to get rid of her inner pain. All her cuts and scars just mask her true identity.

Lynsey, a sophomore in high school, had a very abusive father. No matter how hard she tried, she could never gain his approval, so one day she just stopped trying. Soon she found the acceptance she craved in her first real boyfriend, a senior football player at her school. From the beginning of their relationship, she told him she didn't want to have sex until she got married, but he kept pressuring her. Eventually, she broke up with him. Then, a couple of weeks later, he and his teammates got drunk, found her, and raped her. Ever since then, she's been afraid to say no to the guys she dates, even though she doesn't want to have sex. Now she believes she's worthless, just as her father always said she was.

Emily, who attends a college on the East Coast, was sexually abused by her brother while she was growing up, raped by her first boyfriend in ninth grade, and raped again at a party in college by a guy who she thought was her friend. Now she believes that this is what she was made for. Every morning when she wakes up, the memory of abortion and the reality of a sexually transmitted disease reinforce this lie.

In every one of these cases, no one at their school knew what these students had been through. I was the first person they told their story to. Marianne said that she didn't want anyone at her school to know her secret. "The people here are so different from me," she said. "If they knew this part of me, they wouldn't like me. No one would want to be around me if they knew the truth."

So many of us think this way. We're afraid of what others will think of us, so we hide behind a mask. But if you wear a mask long enough, eventually you'll come to believe the lie that it's the real you. You may fool others and even your-self, but you can't fool God. He knows who you really are, and He wants you to know too, but that can't happen until you remove your mask.

True freedom is found in being who you really are, who God made you to be. Healing requires you to risk opening yourself up. This may take time. That's okay. Michelangelo didn't free David from his marble prison in a day. God won't force you to take off your mask, and He won't take it off for you. But if you'll let Him, little by little He will help you remove it. Will you allow Him to reveal the masterpiece beneath your mask?

CALLED to CHOOSE

Through Jeremiah, God told the suffering exiles in Babylon what they had to do to receive His grace. It was something they hadn't done before. He told them that they needed to trust Him. They had a choice: They could either trust Him to bring them back from their captivity, or they could depend on the lies of the false prophets to cope with their bondage (Jeremiah 29:8–9).

God is giving you the same choice today. Because sexual abuse robbed you of your power to choose as a child, you may feel as if you've never really had a choice. But you do! You can choose to heal! Are you standing at the crossroad of choice in your life right now, wondering which way to go? This is what the Lord says: "Stand at the crossroads and look; ask for the ancient paths, ask where the good way is, and walk in it, and you will find rest for your souls" (Jeremiah 6:16 NIV). When God shows you the good way—the healing path—will you choose to walk in it?

Healing can't occur in a prison built on the lie that we have the power to protect ourselves from pain by controlling our own life. Healing occurs when we choose to hand control of our life over to God. Anything else leads us right back to where we started, still chained down by the consequences of sexual abuse.

There are no more excuses. You have a choice. God is asking you to choose life by loving Him, obeying Him, and committing yourself firmly to Him. Abundant life is available through His Spirit. You may not know who you really are, but He knows, and He says that you are a person with a hope and a future. He is asking you to hand over control of your life to Him so He can free you and heal you.

I know that life is hard when you think there's no hope that things will get better. But God promises that if you trust Him, things *will* get better. Choose to take Him at His word. Believe that He has a plan for you and the power to carry it out. The more you trust Him and walk with Him along the journey, the more healing He will release into your life.

"IF YOU HOLD ANYTHING AGAINST ANYONE, FORGIVE HIM SO THAT YOUR FATHER IN HEAVEN MAY FORGIVE YOU YOUR SINS."

"IF YOU HOLD ANYTHING AGAINST ANYONE, FORGIVE HIM SO THAT YOUR FATHER IN HEAVEN MAY FORGIVE YOU YOUR SINS."

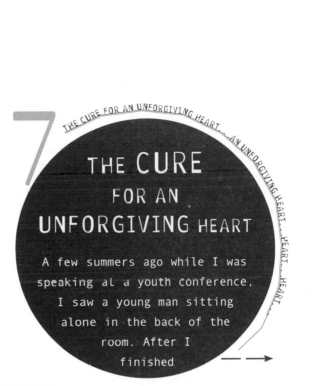

7

THE CURE
FOR AN
UNFORGIVING HEART

A few summers ago while I was speaking at a youth conference, I saw a young man sitting alone in the back of the room. After I finished

— —→

"IF YOU HOLD ANYTHING AGAINST ANYONE, FORGIVE HIM SO THAT YOUR FATHER IN HEAVEN MAY FORGIVE YOU YOUR SINS."

Mark 11:25 NIV

my talk, Cameron spoke to me; but when he did, he wouldn't look me in the eye. He looked at the floor and kept squeezing his hands into fists. His lips were tight. He told me that throughout his childhood his dad had abused both him and his mom and that he hated him for it. He said that his parents were now divorced but that he knew where his dad lived and wanted to kill him. He asked me if God would forgive him.

Forgiving is the third major step to healing from abuse. But like Cameron, we may not want to forgive those who have hurt us. To continue moving forward on our healing journey, we have to understand why it's so important to forgive and how we can find a cure for an unforgiving heart.

REALIZE the REAL PROBLEM

Anger aimed at your abuser is a fitting response to what happened to you. Sexual abuse was an atrocious assault on your body, soul, and spirit, and you have every right to be angry about it. I want you to know that I understand that, for I've been where you are. I want you to know that your feelings and thoughts are normal and valid.

Tell your heavenly Father what you're feeling and thinking. He knows anyway, so just talk to Him about it. Don't shut Him out. Like any good and loving parent, He would rather work it out with you. He won't leave you if you yell at Him—even if you happen to slip a few choice words in there!

God doesn't have a problem with your anger. The only thing He has a problem with is sin. Anger is an emotion, not a decision. Emotions aren't sins, but choosing to act on them can lead to sin. God says, "Don't sin by letting anger control you" (Ephesians 4:26).

My friend Raquel has an older cousin who sexually abused her when she was a child. "In my process of healing," she says, "I came to a personal realization of what sin is and the fact that it separates us from God. If we play around with it, we open up our lives to Satan and his schemes. As I sought healing, I realized that it wasn't my cousin, but my cousin's sin that caused me to suffer. We can look to God to cleanse the sin, and after that He can help us to forgive our abuser."

God has instructed us to commit ourselves to Him. When we do that, we become His children, His property. Therefore, if people violate us, they actually sin against God, not us.

King David recognized this truth after he committed adultery with Bathsheba. In his confession to God, he said, "Against you, and you alone, have I sinned" (Psalm 51:4).

Do you know what God wants to do most when He's sinned against? Kill the guilty person? Take revenge? No! He wants to forgive them (Hebrews 8:12). That's why He sent His Son to die on the cross—so that "everyone who believes in him will have their sins forgiven through his name" (Acts 10:43).

Sin lies behind both our abuse and our failure to forgive our abuser. Since God paid such a high price to be able to forgive those who have sinned against Him, we must also forgive those who have sinned against us.

RECOGNIZE GOD'S STANDARD OF FORGIVENESS

I'm often asked, "Did you forgive your stepdad?" For a long time I thought I had. As a Christian, I believed that it was my *duty* to forgive. I didn't want anyone to view me as unforgiving; I wanted people to see me as a good Christian. I thought they would look down on me if I ever said that I hadn't forgiven my stepdad, or anyone else, for that matter. At the same time, I felt ashamed to think I would ever *not* forgive someone.

I DIDN'T REALLY KNOW WHAT IT MEANT TO FORGIVE.

To be honest, I didn't really know what it meant to forgive. Saying I had done so was easy enough, and for a long time I never felt the need to do anything more than that. I thought I had forgiven my stepdad simply because I believed I had and said I had.

True forgiveness, however, means forgiving with our emotions, our mind, and our will. It's a conscious choice to let go of the need to force our abusers to fix or pay for the mess they have caused in our lives. It's a mental resolve to lay it all at the foot of the cross. It took me a long time to understand what forgiveness really means, but once I did, it changed my life.

During high school and my first year of college, deep within my soul where no one else could see, I didn't truly believe that my stepfather was worthy of forgiveness. I was still harboring a great deal of anger, bitterness, and hatred toward him, and I had no true peace. When I realized this, I began to struggle. I knew that if my relationship with God were as it should be, there would be peace.

By the beginning of my second year of college, I felt that God was speaking to me, telling me that it was time to let go and allow Him to mend my heart. The time had come to look forward, not back. I didn't want my past to affect my future in negative ways. I wanted to allow God to fully heal me so I could be everything He created me to be and do everything He called me to do. At that time I fully laid it all down before Him. And when I did, the Lord showed me what I already knew deep inside: I needed to truly forgive my stepfather.

After I came to this realization, I spent some serious time in prayer. I set aside moments of silence. I journaled. All of this led up to a life-changing moment one morning during fall semester of my sophomore year.

I was lying on the bottom bunk in my dorm room. The building I lived in that year was very old, and the heating system clanked away all day and all night. It was always so hot in our rooms that we all kept our windows open in order to keep the temperature bearable. I remember that I had fallen asleep while deep in prayer the night before. Just as I began to wake up that morning, I felt a fresh breeze on my face from the open window next to my head. In that moment, I felt as if God was breathing new life into me. I kept my eyes shut, basking in His presence.

As I lay there with my eyes shut, in my mind's eye I saw the Lord and my stepdad standing next to each other. The Lord was on the right; my stepdad was on the left. Vince wouldn't look at the Lord, but the Lord was looking directly at him. I could sense that He was very angry about what my stepfather had done to me.

Then I saw the Lord turn around. Now His back was to my stepdad, and He was facing me. Vince was behind the Lord and couldn't see me, and I felt safe because the Lord was directly between us. As the Lord and I looked at each other, I saw Him begin to cry. Soon He was sobbing because of how His precious, innocent child had been abused. He was hurting because I was hurting. He fell to His knees. I ran into His arms, and He held me as we cried together.

And then I saw that behind us my stepdad was also kneeling. He was repenting, tugging on the hem of the Lord's robe, crying out for mercy and forgiveness for everything he had done. Then I saw the Lord forgive my stepfather. And just as quickly as He forgave, He turned back to comfort me.

That breezy morning was a turning point for me. I believe that God was asking me to make a decision that day. I knew that He had forgiven me, and now I knew that what I had just seen was also true: He would also forgive my stepdad. I knew that if anyone—*anyone*—repents and asks the Lord to forgive him of his sin, God would do it that instant. That morning, as the sun was shining on my face and the curtains of my dorm room flapped up and down in the wind, I said to myself, *I'm not above God. I must forgive, just as He does.*

You may never have an experience like this in which the Lord *shows* you that you need to forgive your abuser. God wants to have a personal relationship with His children, and He reveals Himself to each of us in ways He knows will work for us. He knows that I'm a visual person, so He often uses visions like this to teach and guide me. God always speaks to us through His Word, but He might reinforce His message through a song on the radio, a sermon in church, an article in a magazine—or even through this book! The Spirit of God knows the very best way to speak to each one of us.

I'M NOT ABOVE GOD. I MUST FORGIVE, JUST AS HE DOES.

To all of us, the Lord says: "Do not judge others, and you will not be judged. For you will be treated as you treat others. The standard you use in judging is the standard by which you will be judged" (Matthew 7:1–2). I'm so thankful that God forgave me based on His standard instead of the one I used all the years I thought my stepdad wasn't worthy of forgiveness.

RELINQUISH THE RIGHT TO REVENGE

Cameron not only didn't want to forgive his father; he wanted to kill him. He wanted revenge. I want you to know that the need to see justice done is also normal. How do I know that? Because we are made in the image of God, and God is as just as He is merciful. He not only *will* punish sin; He *must* punish it.

Just as Christ's death freed you from your sins, it freed you from the need for revenge. He has promised you that justice will be done. "Dear friends, never take revenge. Leave that to the righteous anger of God. For the Scriptures say, 'I will take revenge; I will pay them back,' says the Lord" (Romans 12:19). The question is, do you believe Him? If you do, will you choose to let go of your right to revenge?

I remember reading a story of how the people living in small villages in India used to catch monkeys. They would place a banana in a jar and bury it, leaving only the mouth of the jar exposed. Then they would hide and wait for a monkey to come along. When one did, he would reach into the mouth of the jar, which was just wide enough for his empty hand to squeeze through. The monkey would clutch the fruit and then try to pull it out, only to find that he couldn't as long as he was holding on to it.

When the hunters showed up, the monkey would try to run away, but since he needed his hands to run, he couldn't escape as long as he was holding on to the banana. The monkey would jump and howl, but he wouldn't let go of that banana. As a result, he was doomed to spend the rest of his life in a cage.

When we hang on to our right to revenge, we lose our freedom just like that monkey. Letting go of our rights and holding on instead to Jesus' promises frees us to move on with life. When we open our fist, let go of our rights, and remove our hand from the jar, we give God total control to make things right. Only then do we allow genuine healing to flow into our lives.

REBUKE SATAN'S LIES

I've received numerous e-mails from students who say they still feel guilty for things they've done in their lives. Even though they've asked for forgiveness, they don't *feel* forgiven. Unless we experience God's forgiveness in our own life, we can't freely offer it to others. Satan, the ultimate abuser, will do his best to see that you don't forgive yourself or others.

God wants you to *know* you're forgiven. He says that we are completely forgiven because Jesus "forgave all our sins" (Colossians 2:13). *All* of them! Satan, on the other hand, wants you to feel unforgiven, condemned. He knows that if you feel guilty and ashamed, you'll think you're separated from God. If you believe Satan, he wins.

When you feel unforgiven, even though there's no basis for this feeling, go back to the truth. God's Word will remind you that the blood of Jesus makes you completely pure and holy (2 Peter 1:9). Believe that God's Word is true. Trust that He is working and wants to cleanse the thoughts and emotions that feed your unforgiving heart. Take captive every thought (2 Corinthians 10:5) and don't trust your natural understanding (Proverbs 3:5). Put your faith in the Word of God: You are forgiven!

Just as Satan doesn't want you to forgive yourself, he doesn't want you to forgive others. Saying "I will never be able to forgive that person" gives Satan glory for his deceit and lies. You may not be ready to forgive today, but that's different from being unable to ever forgive. If you truly want to heal, you *must* forgive, not for your abuser's sake, but for your sake.

> UNFORGIVINGNESS DOESN'T HURT THE ONE WHO HARMED YOU; IT ONLY HURTS YOU.

Unforgivingness doesn't hurt the one who harmed you; it only hurts *you*. No wonder it's Satan's preferred tool to keep abuse survivors in bondage! If we allow him to feed our unforgiving spirit, we'll never experience the power that forgiveness has to set us free. Forgiveness will tear down the walls that imprison us, but we can't know that until we try it. Satan would like to keep us from ever trying. Outsmart the Enemy by standing firmly on God's promises. Rebuke Satan's lies! Forgive.

REMEMBER what JESUS SAID

When Jesus hung on the cross, He said, "Father, forgive them, for they don't know what they are doing" (Luke 23:34).

Olivia scheduled a one-on-one session with me after I spoke at her college. She told me that her babysitter had been sexually abused when she was five and that she in turn had abused Olivia when she babysat her years later. She said that during my talk the light went on in her head, and she began to understand a little bit about why her babysitter had done what she had. "Until now I've been totally unwilling to forgive her," Olivia said. "But after what you said about how hurting people often hurt others, I feel a little more willing." She wanted to know how to take the next step.

"In my case," Raquel told me, "my cousin was caught up in pornography and impure sexual thoughts at an early age, and I was a victim because of it. He used me because I was little and probably thought I would be easy to keep silent. He took advantage of my innocence and hurt me. What he did was wrong, and it was horrible to go through; but I've recognized that he was a hurting kid when he molested me and that he was confused."

Remember that no matter what happened to your abuser in her own childhood or what was going on in his life when he abused you, it was *not* okay for them to take it out on you. Nevertheless, you may be more willing to forgive when you realize that there's no way you can know everything that was going on in your abuser's life or what motivated him to do what he did.

Paul said, "Don't make judgments about anyone ahead of time— before the Lord returns. For he will bring our darkest secrets to light and will reveal our private motives" (1 Corinthians 4:5). Christ alone knows your abuser's heart and all that he's been through, and only He is in a position to judge him. All He calls you to do is to forgive. "The central reason I have chosen to forgive my cousin," Raquel said, "is because I know he is worthy of forgiveness, just as you and I are."

Jesus had a lot to say about forgiveness, and some of it is very hard for us to hear. Although it may seem impossible at times, there's just no way around it. The Lord says: "If you forgive those who sin against you, your heavenly Father will forgive you.

But if you refuse to forgive others, your Father will not forgive your sins" (Matthew 6:14–15). This is the answer to the question Cameron asked me that day after chapel. Forgiving others is as important as having our own sins forgiven.

Letting go of anger and the desire for revenge is the cure for an unforgiving heart. Understanding what forgiving truly means and why it's so important prepare you to release everything that has kept an unforgiving spirit alive within you. I believe that your decision to forgive will come at the perfect time in your healing process, after you've let it all go. I also believe that you'll know it's time because you'll have a burning desire to forgive your abuser as God has forgiven you.

REMEMBER, THE LORD FORGAVE YOU, SO YOU MUST FORGIVE OTHERS.
REMEMBER, THE LORD FORGAVE YOU, SO YOU MUST FORGIVE OTHERS.

REMEMBER, THE LORD FORGAVE YOU, SO YOU MUST FORGIVE OTHERS.

8

CUTTING
THE CORD

Have you ever seen a mother
walking around the mall with
a child connected to her by a
coiled cord with Velcro wrist
straps at each end?

$\longrightarrow$

REMEMBER,

THE LORD

FORGAVE YOU,

SO YOU MUST

FORGIVE OTHERS.

Colossians 3:13

Although it can be a funny sight, it might help you visualize what I'm talking about with regard to forgiveness.

When you're holding on to the past by not forgiving the one who has wronged you, it's as if you're connected to that person with one of those kiddy leashes. Even if your abuser is no longer around and you'll never see him again, he still controls where you go and what you do. You may even feel as if he is still abusing you in subtle and silent ways.

If that's the case, it's time to cut the cord with the scissors of forgiveness.

In the last chapter we looked at the *why* of forgiveness; now let's focus on the *how*. I know that forgiving is difficult. It may feel like you'll never arrive at the point of forgiveness. Or it may feel impossible to ever forgive completely. Nevertheless, there are some very practical ways we can go about it.

FORGIVING IN THE HEART

One obstacle to forgiving your abuser can be the belief that you must confront him. You may be asking, "What if he doesn't even know how much he hurt me?" or "What if she isn't even remorseful for what she's done?" Don't let this false belief keep you from forgiving. The person who abused you doesn't have to be present or have any part in your forgiveness. If forgiveness had to be done in person, I would never have been able to forgive my stepfather, because he was six feet deep in the ground. You can forgive your abuser in your heart.

You could begin by praying to the Lord in general terms, saying simply that you forgive and release the one who has hurt you. It's important to ask God to reveal anyone He might want you to specifically name and forgive. If He shows you someone, you should forgive and release that person.

Journaling is a great idea. Writing down your thoughts and feelings will help you, both now and in the future when you look back at what you've written. Address someone you feel has really let you down—a parent, sibling, friend, or even God. Write down how he or she hurt you, or make a sketch and then explain it in writing. Try to let yourself go in this process of release. Cry as long and as deeply as you need to.

THE PERSON WHO ABUSED YOU DOESN'T HAVE TO BE PRESENT OR HAVE ANY PART IN YOUR FORGIVENESS.

When you're ready to forgive, you could write to your abuser. Even though my stepfather was no longer alive, I wrote him a letter. I let it all out, and I let it all go. Peace, joy, and love instantly filled my soul, driving out all my feelings of anger, despair, humiliation, and betrayal. I can't explain how it happened other than by agreeing with Paul that it was the work of the Holy Spirit. "The Holy Spirit produces this kind of fruit in our lives: love, joy, peace, patience, kindness, goodness, faithfulness, gentleness, and self-control" (Galatians 5:22–23).

If you aren't ready to forgive right now and don't want to commit to writing something you don't really mean, take a different route. God wants you to be honest. He already knows what is in your heart, so you don't need to hide anything. Tell Him that you aren't ready. Share your thoughts, your fears, and your frustrations about forgiving those who have hurt you. Just lay it all out there for Him.

As you talk to God about it, acknowledge that you know that His Word says that you must forgive despite your feelings and fears. Tell Him that because of that, you choose to forgive by placing all your hurt and resentment in His hands. Trust Him to take it from you immediately, and then ask Him to let you begin to feel the freedom that forgiveness brings. I believe this is the kind of honest prayer that God longs to hear and that He will make that release real to you.

Another thing you can do is to pray for your abuser. "My karate instructor sexually abused me when I was seven," James told me. "I went to counseling and dealt with some of that, but after you spoke at chapel service last semester, I felt convicted about my unforgiving spirit. I knew it was from some of the anger and bitterness I still felt inside.

"That day, I made a decision to pray for thirty days for the man who had wronged me. I didn't pray that he would face God's judgment or that he would see where he was wrong. Instead, I asked God to bless and prosper his life—which was really hard to do! As the month came to an end, I noticed my attitude beginning to change. Sometimes I actually *meant* what I was praying for! I believe it's impossible to harbor bad thoughts about someone at the same time you're earnestly praying for them. This was a big step toward my healing."

It's easy to pray for the victimized of the world, but praying for those responsible can be very difficult. I've met with many students who refuse to pray for their abuser. "She doesn't deserve my prayers," they say. Or "I don't want God to bless his life. He deserves bad and pain for all he did." I understand their feelings because I once felt the same way. I hated my stepdad so much that I didn't even want to see him in heaven. Nevertheless, God expects us to forgive those who have hurt us.

FORGIVING FACE-TO-FACE

While some of you can't or don't want to confront your abuser, others of you may want to do this in order to bring his sin into the light before you offer forgiveness. It's quite possible that your abuser is still alive. You may even see him from time to time. You might have had a decent relationship in the past and believe there's a potential to fix what's been broken. Some of you may even be at a point where you want to try to restore the relationship. Directly confronting an abuser isn't something every survivor is prepared to take on, but for those who are, it can be a dramatic, cleansing experience for both victim and abuser.

However, if you decide to forgive face-to-face, you need to be very careful. Confrontation can sometimes be unrealistic or even downright dangerous. If you think that confronting your abuser is something you need to do, pray about it, speak to a counselor, and ask someone to go with you. Consider every angle before you move ahead, and when you do, walk carefully. When you're dealing with an abusive person, be careful not to jump into a personal confrontation without prayerfully preparing yourself and considering the various ways the situation could unfold. Always, always, *always* remember to pray in advance of any confrontation and to have others praying during the meeting as well.

Forgiving face-to-face may not be a one-time conversation. It may be an ongoing process of reaching out to the one who hurt you, shedding light into the darkness of his life, and offering forgiveness. I would encourage you to bring a friend with you to these meetings. It's important to have someone present as a witness and to support you. This person doesn't have to say anything during the confrontation; she doesn't even need to be in the same room. She can just sit in the car and pray for you or sit at an adjacent table in a restaurant where you plan to meet your abuser.

Successful confrontation involves a rebuke on your part and repentance on your abuser's part. This means it can't occur until your abuser is able to admit his wrongdoing without placing blame anywhere but on himself. When you confront him, you need to rebuke his sin against you and invite him to repent. If he is truly repentant, and if you're ready to move into a place of reconciliation, you have an opportunity to begin to build a new relationship.

SUCCESSFUL CONFRONTATION INVOLVES A REBUKE ON YOUR PART AND REPENTANCE ON YOUR ABUSER'S PART.

Explain your thoughts and feelings and ask your abuser to express his about what happened in the past and about his current relationship (or lack of relationship) with you. All of this is best done in a meeting with a counselor present to act as a mediator and guide the conversation. This is something you and a counselor can prepare for months in advance to ensure that you have considered all possible outcomes and are ready.

Confrontations often don't work out as planned. This can be a letdown. "When my family learned that my cousin had abused me, we confronted him," Raquel told me.

"He didn't admit that what he had done was wrong. To this day, he still hasn't. He has always said that we were both experimenting. That was hard for me as I grew up, especially at family reunions."

Even if you're able to walk with your abuser through rebuke and repentance and then move in the direction of a restored relationship, you'll likely encounter some shadowy valleys along the road. It's possible to forgive the one who has hurt you, yet still be suspicious and careful of him. Offering him forgiveness doesn't mean you automatically have to trust him. You must be gracious, but smart—or as the Lord put it, "wise as serpents and harmless as doves" (Matthew 10:16 NKJV).

Don't think you must trust this person to the point that he can hurt you again. Unfortunately, there are people in this world who, no matter what we do or say, will continue to hurt us every chance they get. If you're never able to completely trust your abuser, you won't ever be able to have a healthy relationship with him.

After having tried everything she knew to restore her relationship with her stepbrother, Darcy accepted the fact that for her to heal and move on, she was going to have to make a clean break with him. "Forgiveness of an act and acceptance of an act are two different things," she said. "I tried to work things out with Brandon, but every time I try, he just twists my words, pulls me into his control again, makes me feel guilty, and hurts me even more. Trying to get him to admit his wrong and repent hasn't worked, and fortunately God showed me that."

Darcy harbors no bitterness or desire for revenge, but she knows she can't fully trust Brandon until she sees some change. She has had to accept that no matter what she says, he will probably never admit his wrongdoing or respond to her in the way she needs and wants him to. She has told him that if he truly wants to participate in the process of repentance and renewal, their severed relationship can be reversed. Darcy prays this will happen, but until it does, the only thing she can do is to forgive him in her heart.

If your abuser is unremorseful, I would pass it off as another control tactic. The way I respond to this kind of attitude is to freely offer forgiveness. This might seem directly the opposite of what you'd expect. However, my reasoning is simple. If you conclude that someone isn't worthy of grace, you give him power and authority in your life that he doesn't deserve. People like that want to control you, and if they can make you decide not to forgive them, they get what they want. What you get is a lifetime in a prison of pain.

No matter what the outcome is when you attempt to forgive your abuser face-to-face, remind yourself that you deserve the best. You deserve the truth; you deserve safety and happiness. If, after you've made honest attempts, your abuser won't repent and work toward a right relationship with you, remember that forgiveness doesn't have to be done face-to-face.

FORGIVING ENABLERS AND YOURSELF

Forgiveness isn't only about forgiving those who have abused us. Many times there are people in our lives who, though they weren't the actual abusers, knew about the abuse and did nothing stop it. This can be just as damaging as the abuse itself. The belief that we weren't important enough to protect is a very real issue that survivors silently struggle with. If you believe that lie, begin by replacing it with these truths:

You ought to have been able TO TRUST the ADULTS in your life!

You were SUPPOSED to have someone STAND UP for you!

You should have been PROTECTED!

When those people failed to believe and protect you, they made a bad choice, and they will reap the consequences. But you have suffered long enough. Now it's time to move beyond that. Your thoughts and feelings about those who enabled your abuser need healing too, and forgiveness is the key to doing that.

Someone else you may need to forgive is yourself. It's common for survivors to act in sinful ways because of our abuse. Many times we make wrong choices as a direct result of the pain we feel or of what we have been taught. The consequences of our harmful choices can range anywhere from making an incredible mess of our lives to just making us feel uncomfortable. Whatever the result, if we want to experience peace, we will need to forgive ourselves.

YOUR THOUGHTS AND FEELINGS ABOUT THOSE WHO ENABLED YOUR ABUSER NEED HEALING TOO.

When Renée was fourteen, she found the courage to tell her foster mother that her foster father had been abusing her. Her foster mother told her to "hush," and the next morning Renée ran away. She began using drugs and within weeks was addicted. With her money running out, she needed a job, and one of her drug dealers told her he could help her make lots of easy money. That night she entered the dark, degrading lifestyle of a teenage prostitute. "Back then," she said, "I felt so dirty and worthless, so I just told myself it didn't matter."

A few months later, Renée accepted Christ as her Lord and Savior, and He rescued her from her pit. With the help of her new church family, she got treatment for her drug addiction and began the healing journey from sexual abuse. Even though her future now looked bright, Renée still felt great shame. While she accepted that God had already forgiven her, she still needed to forgive herself. This was the only way she could free herself from the past and move on to the future God had waiting for her.

In my own case, as an adolescent I behaved badly toward my biological father, Gary. It wasn't anything dramatic, but I knew it wasn't right. My stepfather said things about my real dad that made me believe he was a bad father. His comments, just like Satan's lies, took root in my mind, and I pushed my dad away and said things about him that weren't always true. Although my father had never done anything wrong, I was too scared to admit that my stepdad was abusing me, so I thought it would be safer to project my feelings onto my real dad.

When the truth about the abuse finally came out, my father told me that I could share with him what I wanted to, but that he didn't need to know everything. He said he just wanted to be there for me—and he was. I felt horrible for how I had treated him as a result of my relationship with my abusive,

The starting point of forgiving yourself is to confess your sin and ask the Lord to forgive you.

lying stepdad, and I realized that I needed to tell him I was sorry. He forgave me without question. However, I continued to beat myself up for treating him badly. Eventually, I realized that I also had to forgive myself. Once I understood why I had acted as I did, it was easy.

The starting point of forgiving yourself is to confess your sin and ask the Lord to forgive you. He promises that "if we confess our sins to him, he is faithful and just to forgive us our sins and to cleanse us from all wickedness" (1 John 1:9). It's helpful to have a knowledgeable friend, prayer partner, pastor, or professional Christian counselor pray and talk with you during the process of forgiveness and release. Allow others to come alongside to listen or pray for you.

On your healing journey, confessing your sin can help hold you accountable, and sharing your act of forgiveness with a trusted individual can encourage you. If you don't have someone who can help you with this right now, don't worry! Forgiveness is an incredible act that can be done in your heart, just between you and God. You don't need anyone else to witness it or tell you that you have it right or wrong.

GETTING OFF the HOOK

Forgiving someone who has wronged you isn't the same as excusing him for what he has done or saying that what he did was okay. The one you choose to forgive may never change. But don't worry. Cutting the cord that binds you to your abuser never means letting him off the hook. You simply hand him over to God. He will take care of things from there. He is the final Judge, and now it's His business, not yours.

When I forgave my stepdad, I wasn't letting him off the hook for all the pain he had caused in my life. I was getting myself off the hook by freeing myself from the pain. Forgiving him was about releasing me from all the negative feelings that were keeping me chained to the past. My stepdad gained nothing from this, but I gained life, love, freedom, happiness—and more!

This isn't to say that once you forgive, you'll also forget. You may never forget pieces of your past. Paul never forgot that he had persecuted Christians (1 Corinthians 15:9) or that Jews had persecuted him (2 Corinthians 11:24–25). Nevertheless, he didn't dwell on the past. He knew where his focus should be: "I press on to reach the end of the race and receive the heavenly prize for which God, through Christ Jesus, is calling us" (Philippians 3:14).

God wants us to free ourselves from whatever cord keeps us bound to our past and our abusers. But in order to do that, we must forgive. By acknowledging the damage done and then forgiving those responsible, we free ourselves to deal with the hurt and go on to greater things in life.

HE HIMSELF GIVES LIFE AND BREATH TO EVERYTHING, AND HE SATISFIES EVERY NEED.
HE HIMSELF GIVES LIFE AND BREATH TO EVERYTHING, AND HE SATISFIES EVERY NEED.

HE HIMSELF GIVES LIFE AND BREATH TO EVERYTHING, AND HE SATISFIES EVERY NEED.

9

ALL YOU
NEED

Most of the questions high
school and college students
ask me have to do with
relationships. Was it hard
for you to date? they ask.

HE HIMSELF

GIVES LIFE AND

BREATH TO EVERYTHING,

AND HE SATISFIES

EVERY NEED.

Acts 17:25

"Is it possible to feel safe with a man?" "Will I ever trust anyone again?"

Relationships are often the ultimate test of healing. How well we do in them reveals a lot about how far we've come on our healing journey, as well as what areas still pose problems for us. Looking back, I can see that the struggles I've had on my own journey have almost always shown their faces in my relationships.

Childhood sexual abuse is completely devastating. It encompasses all areas of life and manifests itself in lies that can destroy our ability to relate to others in healthy ways. As adult survivors of abuse, we often don't understand how to have healthy relationships.

The first thing we have to do is to root out the false beliefs that stand in the way. By now, this should sound very familiar. Just as we have to stop believing lies about God and ourselves in order to heal, we must also recognize and root out the lies we believe about others and the world.

WHERE our NEEDS LIE

As children, we can see the world only as far as our little feet can take us. Unfortunately, when our small world is made up of dysfunctional adults and traumatic experiences, we tend to think that's what everyone's world looks like. Having grown up in an abusive environment, our concept of reality can be skewed. "When your innocence is stolen from you in childhood by someone you trust, like your very own father," Melissa says, "you'll never look at the world the same way again."

What survivors of childhood abuse believe about others and the world is based on what was once very true for them. The belief that the world isn't safe was reality for

Melissa as a child. Everyone she loved and trusted had hurt her. When she grew up and left home, her world changed, and this belief was no longer true. However, she continued to make major life decisions as if it were. What had once helped her survive an abusive childhood now hindered her in her relationships.

As we get older and learn about other people's lives, we eventually learn that not everyone lived in a world just like ours. Nevertheless, part of the baggage we often carry with us into adulthood is a suitcase full of lies like these:

NOBODY is safe.
Nobody will protect me.

NOBODY can be trusted.
Nobody wants to be around me.

NOBODY can understand me.
Nobody cares about my needs.

NOBODY could love me.

These beliefs are lies beaten into a child's mind about the most precious thing God has given us: love. From the moment we are violated, we will ask, "Is love real? What does it mean? Is it always selfish?" Because of our abuser's awful sin, we now connect love with shame, betrayal, and hurt.

If we never step out of our dark closet, we'll continue to believe and act on these lies, and we'll never know what love really means or how to have healthy relationships. We'll never know what it's like to feel safe or to be able to trust. We'll remain wounded survivors who base our relationships on the false expectation that others can meet all our emotional needs.

As you allow God to work in your life, He will show you that there are people who will love, protect, help, and understand you; and you'll find yourself becoming emotionally and spiritually stronger. But most of all, you'll come to realize that God Himself is the only One who can satisfy your deepest needs.

THE NEED TO FEEL SAFE

My freshman year of high school began just one month after my stepfather committed suicide. In August I began practice with the junior varsity volleyball team, and a couple of weeks later school began. I was so excited at the prospect of having a normal teenage life! However, all the hurt and mistrust associated with my abuse had now surfaced, and I felt vulnerable. I craved safety.

Not long after the volleyball season began, I noticed some upperclassmen who all sat together on the left side of the gymnasium, straight across the court from our bench. Those guys never missed a home game, so my teammates and I quickly got to know them. One of them paid a lot of attention to me. Brian was thoughtful, respectful, and sweet, and he captured my heart with his humor and his bright smile. But I wasn't ready to date him. I was still afraid of guys.

Then one fall morning when most of us kids were hanging out at our lockers waiting for the bell to ring for first period, I heard a rumor flying down the hall. Kids were saying that the real reason my stepfather had committed suicide was that he had been sexually abusing me. Even though it was true, no one was supposed to know! It hit me like a brick.

Later I found that the source of the rumor was Craig, a boy I had considered a friend. That morning when he walked past me with a group of other boys, he called me "Daddy's girl." My heart fell to the floor. A few of the others were laughing with him, and they all chimed in: "Daddy's girl! Daddy's girl!"

I was very embarrassed, but I didn't want to make matters worse, so I just angrily denied the accusation and tried my best to act tough, as if it didn't bother me at all. But deep down it did. It really did. I was hurting, and it didn't take long before I confided in Brian. Before I could get the whole story out, the bell rang. Brian put his arm around my shoulders and walked me to my first-period class.

I plopped down in my seat and pulled out my chemistry notebook and the homework I had completed the night before. I told myself to just focus on class. But in a matter of seconds, the kids coming into class were turning around and running back out into the hallway. I shot up out of my seat and followed them. There was a fight!

That wasn't too out of the ordinary . . . except that the instigator was Brian! No one could believe it. He was such a good kid, a model student. But today he had decided to defend my honor with his fists. By the beginning of second period, Craig was nursing his wounds, and Brian was officially my boyfriend.

It seems pretty obvious what I was longing for at that time: someone who would stand up for me, protect me, and make me feel safe and secure. Brian was the first guy to do that for me, and I clung to him. I believe that God put Brian in my life at that particular time for many reasons. One of the biggest was to prove to me that it was possible to feel safe with a man.

Trust is a huge issue for those of us who were betrayed

THE NEED FOR TRUST

God also used Brian to help expose the lie that men can't be trusted, a belief I had developed at a very vulnerable stage of my life. Trust is a huge issue for those of us who were betrayed in childhood by those we trusted most. I have spoken with many college guys who are close friends or in a serious dating relationship with a female abuse survivor. They often ask me, "How many times do I have to prove myself to her?"

A boyfriend may be very consistent in being on time and calling if he's going to be late, but if he's late and doesn't call just one time, the mind of an abuse victim will skip over all the evidence that he is trustworthy. Instead, it will zero in on the incident that was the exception to the rule. That's the way your mind works when your core beliefs are rooted in trauma and entrenched since childhood. It looks for evidence that supports the false belief and ignores evidence that contradicts it. "You were late and didn't call; I knew I couldn't trust you." When adult survivors of sexual abuse haven't experienced healing, they will zoom in on others' missteps and have a hard time forgetting about them.

I know this is hard for those of you who care for a survivor of sexual abuse. All I can say to you is "Hang in there! Keep proving yourself." From my own experience, I know that godly men who never stop trying to be trustworthy make a huge impact on the lives of survivors who need to be able to trust men.

Two years after my stepfather's suicide, God brought my mom a new husband and me a new stepdad. Mark was a blessing straight from the Father to both my mom and me, and he played a vital role in helping me dispel the false beliefs I had about men. I needed someone who would show me time and time again that he loved me unconditionally and who would live a holy life in thought, word, and deed. Mark is such a man: trustworthy, safe, stable, genuine, full of moral integrity and truth. I'm so thankful for the many godly men like Mark who help survivors learn to trust without even knowing they're doing it.

While we need to have godly men in our lives, we also need to remember that these wonderful people aren't the ones who complete our healing. In my relationship with Brian, I think I was not only depending on him to protect me, but also expecting him to help heal me. While it was redeeming to have someone stick up for me the way he did, I needed to understand that he wasn't the source of my healing.

It's true that others can help in the healing process and at times even play a major role in it. But healing can't happen through them. Healing has to happen in you and through you, with Jesus as the source. Brian couldn't fix the wounds that caused me to fear men. No one could heal those wounds except the Lord.

As the Lord heals your core beliefs, you'll find that there are people you can trust. But most of all, you'll learn that you can trust God. Once you accept this, the little things like your boyfriend always being on time won't faze you anymore.

THE NEED FOR BALANCE AND BOUNDARIES

I've found that Satan likes to attack us in our relationships by toying with our emotions. This is where he can really cause turmoil in our lives. Peter says, "Stay alert! Watch out for your great enemy, the devil. He prowls around like a roaring lion, looking for someone to devour" (1 Peter 5:8). If we don't want to be Satan bait, we need to have relationships that are emotionally balanced.

Part of the healing process involves learning how to negotiate emotional as well as physical space in relationships. Some of us are too distant (disengaged) in relationships. Others are too close (enmeshed). We have to learn what is healthy in terms of spending time with and apart from people we care about.

One young woman I met while speaking at a college in the Northwest touched my heart in a special way. Sara was talented, bright, and creative, but also incredibly wounded by years of severe sexual, physical, and emotional abuse. A friendship developed between us, and I felt the Lord leading me to invest greatly in her life. I helped her get her feet planted in schoolwork and counseling, and I supported her spiritually, emotionally, and even financially at times. We became like sisters.

Sara had very deep wounds, and I felt her pain. I tried to be the hands and feet of Christ to her as I showed her His love. I wanted to make everything okay for her. I wanted to fix her. So I gave and gave and gave.

IF WE DON'T WANT TO BE SATAN BAIT, WE NEED TO HAVE RELATIONSHIPS THAT ARE EMOTIONALLY BALANCED.

I became so consumed with our relationship and Sara's well-being that it took every ounce of my energy every day. And even that never seemed to be enough. Our relationship was unbalanced.

Although I didn't realize it at the time, I was trying to be God in Sara's life. By being what I thought was a good friend and ministering the Lord's love to her, I caused her to put her trust in me instead of in the Lord.

Close friendships are important. It's healthy and biblical to have close friends. But when you think you can be the answer to someone else's problems and make her life worthwhile, something is wrong. God is the One she needs. When you need another person to bring you happiness, something is wrong. God is the One you need. No friend in the world can be to you what God is to you.

Just like balance, boundaries are essential for healthy relationships. It isn't unusual for survivors to struggle with this. Proper boundaries are instilled in us as children. When they were violated in our childhood, the result was devastating. We learned that nothing is sacred and that anything goes. Even our bodies weren't our own!

The lack of healthy boundaries can wreak havoc on our relationships. I see evidence of unhealthy or missing boundaries in the lives of many young men and women I talk with on college campuses and at church conferences. In their relationships, boundaries are usually nonexistent or unclear.

"I was sexually abused as a young girl and never was able to get a hold on my overwhelming emotions," Rose said. "I wasn't able to confront people or set any personal boundaries in relationships, and I had unhealthy attachments to older people in authority, like my boss. I also built up so many walls to protect myself that I sabotaged new friendships. I almost lost my job. I hated myself and made a mess of my life. I knew I needed therapy, so I went."

Setting healthy boundaries is difficult for those who've never known what it means to have them, and like Rose, you may need a counselor to help you. However, any advice a counselor gives you needs to be rooted firmly in what God has to say about how we should relate to others. Our relationships will be truly healthy only when we obey Him in this area.

Getting out of unhealthy relationships is just as important as staying in healthy ones. If others are trying to control your life, if they aren't listening to you, if they are pushing you beyond your boundaries, if they aren't building you up or loving you the way God would want—get out!

THE NEED TO BE UNDERSTOOD

The silence that surrounds sexual abuse makes us feel that others can't understand our pain. Though we have a great longing to be understood, we have an even greater fear of revealing our deep dark secret. This takes a toll on our closest relationships because it prevents others from giving us the understanding we need.

Anytime two people enter into a relationship, they bring with them a lifetime of experiences that shape how they interact with each other. Problems in a relationship often arise when one person doesn't understand why the other reacts to certain situations the way he or she does. This can be very evident when victims of sexual abuse hide their past from a loved one.

Lish and Jake had been dating for six months. On weekends she often went to his bachelor pad to help him with his weekly cleaning. One Sunday, Jake took the garbage out while Lish washed the dishes. When he walked back into the apartment, he sneaked up behind her and gave her a big bear hug to show her how much he appreciated her help. Instead of reacting with a laugh and a kiss as Jake expected, Lish screamed, told him to never do that again, and ran out of the room in tears.

Lish had never told Jake that she had been sexually abused as a child or that his ways of expressing his affection often triggered her terrifying memories. Since Jake didn't know that Lish was a survivor, her reaction left him feeling confused and angry. He interpreted Lish's reactions as a reflection of her feelings about him, and unable to predict how she would react, he hesitated to show her any affection at all.

Because of the episode in the kitchen and others like it, Lish could feel her relationship with Jake slipping away. Her fear of telling Jake about her past was giving way to the greater fear of losing him. The same secret that Lish believed could end the relationship if she decided to tell was slowly degrading their relationship by her decision *not* to tell.

Lish felt that she was at a crossroads, not only in her relationship with Jake, but also in her relationship with God. Night after night she cried out to Him, sharing more deeply than she ever had. The more she poured out her heart, the more she felt understood. God was filling her needs. The open communication with the Lord was a milestone in both her walk with Him and her healing journey. Because of it, she began to feel more comfortable about telling Jake her secret.

When Lish finally did tell Jake, she experienced the same loving acceptance she had from the Lord. For his part, Jake finally understood that Lish's reactions weren't a reflection of how she felt about him.

Today, Jake and Lish are committed to openly discussing everything in their relationship, including Lish's past. This openness has brought them closer together and laid the groundwork for a successful marriage.

As important as communication is in any relationship, it's crucial if you're a survivor of sexual abuse. The decision to reveal this dark part of your past can be frightening, but your willingness to share your most guarded secret is the very thing that will foster the understanding you so desire. Opening up makes it possible for your loved one to understand you, something every survivor needs.

THE NEED to FEEL COMPLETE

As survivors of abuse, we often look to another person to meet our needs so we'll feel complete. But if we do, we're doomed to be disappointed. The relationship won't last, and when it ends, we'll feel as empty as ever.

The belief that any human being can meet all our needs is a delusion. The truth is that even the most perfect person will fail us. There will always be little things that happen along the way that will inevitably let us down. At times every human being will be insensitive, inconsistent, or unavailable.

Between the ages of three and seven, Mariah was abused by two important men in her life. As a teenager, she craved emotional and physical closeness but, at the same time, she avoided it for fear of being hurt or betrayed again. She had a great need to feel safe, and she didn't trust men.

When Mariah was a sophomore in high school, her softball coach paid special attention to her, and they became close. Coach Teri was the only person Mariah had ever felt safe with. But the more time they spent together, the more obsessed Mariah became with her. She got very jealous when Coach Teri spent extra time with other players, but Mariah didn't want to develop any other relationships because she believed they wouldn't be safe. She depended on her coach to meet not only her need for safety, but all her other emotional needs as well.

In the middle of Mariah's junior year, Coach Teri was offered a coaching position at a college out of state. When she moved away, Mariah was back where she started, still needing closeness, still feeling unsafe, and still mistrusting men. Her attempt to meet all her needs in one single relationship had inevitably failed.

I've met other girls and women who haven't yet accepted the truth that no human relationship can meet all our needs. Even though they have a relationship with, or even marry, a really wonderful guy, the relationship often ends in disaster because expectations like these are too great for anyone but the Lord to meet. No human can give us all we need to feel complete. And if we're honest, we have to admit that deep inside we long for something more. That's how we're made. We have a hole in our heart, a void that only God can fill.

Love is at the heart of our relationships with others, and it is real. How do I know that? Because God is real, and He is love (1 John 4:8). God loves us as no human being ever could, and He wants to be our safety, our comforter, our healer, our satisfaction. If I had looked for all of these things solely in Brian, or in anyone else, I would have experienced only a pinch of what was available to me. Jesus says to "'seek the Kingdom of God above all else, and live righteously, and he will give you everything you need'" (Matthew 6:33).

I'm so thankful I was able to find complete satisfaction in God! He was the only One who could meet all my needs, and as I relied upon Him, my relationships became healthier and prepared me for the most intimate relationship of all—marriage.

DELIGHT YOURSELF IN THE LORD AND HE WILL GIVE YOU THE DESIRES OF YOUR HEART.
DELIGHT YOURSELF IN THE LORD AND HE WILL GIVE YOU THE DESIRES OF YOUR HEART.

DELIGHT YOURSELF IN THE LORD AND HE WILL GIVE YOU THE DESIRES OF YOUR HEART.

10

THE
DESIRES OF
YOUR HEART

After my stepfather committed
suicide, my mom and I moved
back into our home and
completely redecorated the
interior. We focused

— →

DELIGHT

YOURSELF IN THE

LORD, AND HE WILL

GIVE YOU THE

DESIRES OF YOUR HEART.

Psalm 37:4 NIV

on our bedrooms. I went from a pink room covered with ballerinas and kittens to a gray, red, and black room decorated with Chicago Bulls and Ohio State Buckeyes memorabilia. I loved it!

Turning my bedroom into a fresh new space was a symbolic act of cleansing and renewal. Free of abuse, I looked forward to one day having a healthy marriage. Even when I was a little girl, the desire of my heart was to one day get married. I think that might be the desire of your heart as well.

Psalm 37:4 says that if you delight yourself in the Lord, He will give you the desires of your heart. This doesn't mean that if there's anything you want, including a spouse, you'll get it. God gives us what we ask for only if it accords with His will for us (1 John 5:14). If His desire is for you to have a spouse, that will be your desire as well, and He will bring you the one He has chosen for you when the time is right.

FINDING the PERFECT MATE

When I was twelve, I used to lie in bed praying for my future husband. I continued to pray for him until the day I met him. I prayed for God's will in his life, for his safety, and for his purity. I prayed that God would keep him strong in the face of temptation. I prayed that the Lord would prepare him for me, and I asked the Lord to prepare me for him.

My decision to seek counseling in college was based in part on my desire to fully prepare myself for marriage in the future. I didn't want to overlook any woundedness from my childhood or leave any stone unturned in getting ready for what God had in store for me. But even though I never doubted that God was preparing the perfect mate for me, I admit that at times I tried to help Him out a bit.

I was longing for someone who could protect me and rescue me from my issues. When a guy came along who seemed to fit the bill, I asked God to turn him into my future husband and perfect mate. When that didn't seem

FINDING THE RIGHT PERSON ISN'T NEARLY AS IMPORTANT AS BEING THE RIGHT PERSON.

to work, I tried in my own power to change him into what I knew I needed and what I thought God wanted for me. But that didn't work either. In the end, any change I saw in him was the result of his doing it for me.

Some of you may be thinking, *Well, what's wrong with that?* Even though it meant a lot to me that a guy would do what it took to keep me, deep down in my heart I knew that the relationship wouldn't last because it wasn't authentic.

I wanted to marry a man who was the same with or without me. I wanted a man I could trust, a man of integrity, strong moral character, and conviction. I wanted a husband who loved the Lord, who prayed, and who sought His will. I wanted him to show women respect and live a clean and holy life. I longed for a man with a heart full of compassion for others, who wanted to serve God and who would support me in my ministry. And I wanted him to be all of these things *on his own*, without me trying to make him that way. I knew God loved me enough to fulfill my desires by preparing this person for me. I simply needed to let go and trust Him to answer my prayers.

Finding the right person isn't nearly as important as *being* the right person. Many people think that getting married will solve the problems arising from sexual abuse, but it won't. In fact, it often makes them worse! There might be someone who makes you feel good and all tingly inside for a time. But it's only a quick fix, an infatuation. It won't last. Your long-term happiness depends upon having God in your heart, leading your life.

Without the Lord's healing in your life, it will be nearly impossible for you to have a healthy, intimate relationship with the mate God has chosen for you. In my opinion, you shouldn't even be thinking about marriage until you have an intimate relationship with Christ. Jesus said that the first and greatest commandment is to "'love the Lord your God with all your heart, all your soul, and all your mind'" (Matthew 22:37–38). The Lord, not your future spouse, needs to be your focus. Only He can help you overcome the obstacles to intimacy that sexual abuse has placed in your path.

OVERCOMING OBSTACLES TO INTIMACY

Unless you make a commitment to follow the healing path Christ has for you, the trauma of sexual abuse can lead you to engage in sexual relationships that not only prevent you from healing, but also lead to further trauma through sexually transmitted disease, unwanted pregnancies, abortion, or more abuse.

Childhood sexual abuse is extremely devastating to its victims' sense of self-worth, and low self-esteem can perpetuate the cycle of abuse in their lives. Survivors who believe they're worthless are often targeted by controlling people who reinforce that belief. Unfortunately, marrying such people sometimes makes survivors the victims of spousal abuse.

Keirsten's youth pastor sexually abused her. She found the courage to report the abuse, but since she was told to *hush*, she didn't heal as she should have. In college, she dated guys who seemed nice at first, but they all ended up hurting her. Finally, in her junior year she thought she had found the love of her life. Despite the fact that Richard decided who she could spend time with and how long she could spend on the phone with them, his interest in being with her made Keirsten feel important and loved. They got married the next summer.

It didn't take long before Richard's seemingly harmless desire to be with Keirsten all the time cut her completely off from the world. When she made a few attempts to initiate new friendships, the emotional abuse became physical abuse that left her with visible bruises.

Like Keirsten, female survivors who haven't been able to work through the pain of the past can repeatedly hook up with guys who end up breaking their hearts. Often these guys are interested only in sex, not in them. Many of these girls admit that they are attracted to "bad boys." They say they wouldn't put up with physically abusive guys, but they recognize their pattern of dating men who are verbally abusive and selfish.

Somewhere inside, some abuse victims feel unclean and unable to regain their lost purity. Eventually they can become promiscuous, engaging in one-night stands or having multiple sexual partners. Since Tiffany didn't have any sense of self-worth, her life became like a broken record. She would go to a party, meet a new guy, date him for a week or so, sleep with him, and then dump him soon after. *I'm already damaged goods,* she thought. *Who cares how many people I have sex with?*

The answer is that *God* cares. Because sexual relations can have such a huge impact on your healing and your future, God sets a high standard for sexual purity. If you were a victim of childhood sexual abuse, you need to know that you are not damaged goods. What happened to you was not your fault. You didn't choose to have sex back then. But you can choose now.

Starting today, you can choose to make healthy relationship choices, and you can choose purity. I hope you make the right choice. You are worth it, and so is your future. Not trusting God in this area of your life will not only delay your healing, but also prevent you from receiving the answer to your prayers.

RECEIVING the ANSWER TO YOUR PRAYERS

After graduating from high school, I planned to leave my small Ohio town to attend a college just outside of Boston, Massachusetts. This was a tough decision for me, as I was concerned about being so far away from my mother. She knew I was worried, so she wrote me a letter saying that it was time for her to let go and allow me to follow God's plan for my life. That freed me to leave everything I knew to go to the college the Lord had led me to. It was still hard and I was often homesick, but I knew I was where I was supposed to be at the time.

One afternoon I went to the gym for one of my basketball workouts. There was a cute guy sitting on the incline bench in the weight room. Although I'd never met him, I knew who he was. His name was Matt Bromley. He was attending college just outside of Chicago, Illinois; but that weekend he was home visiting his family, who lived near my college. Many of his friends from high school and youth group attended my school, and a couple of them were also my teammates. They spoke of him from time to time, and he was in some of the pictures on their dorm walls.

That day in the gym, we didn't speak or even make eye contact, and I didn't think about the chance encounter again until that evening. I was in my dorm room, doing my nightly devotions and writing in my prayer journal when the Lord spoke to me as clear as day: *You will marry Matt Bromley.* I felt kind of excited about that and recorded it in my journal, but I tried not to think about it too long. I did nothing to initiate a relationship, and in fact, our paths didn't cross again for five years. By then, I had almost forgotten him.

Two years after I graduated from college, Matt and I formally met for the first time. (Yes, ladies, it is possible to find your husband *after* college!) It was a Friday night. I was on the road for a speaking engagement and had made plans to get together with a former college roommate while I was in the area. We hadn't seen each other for more than two years. She was married to Matt's older brother, so she and her husband decided to invite Matt for dinner that night too. Little did we know that they had major life plans for the two of us!

Matt was everything I had prayed for . . . and more. By the end of the weekend, I remembered the journal entry I'd made so long ago, and I felt that for five years God had been preparing us for that very weekend. I had complete peace. I felt complete trust. I had no doubt that Matt was the one for me. Matt just hadn't gotten that message yet!

We dated for almost a year. Then on New Year's Day, 2005, while we were standing on a bridge in New York City's Central Park, Matt told me that he loved me and that he believed I was the one God had chosen for him to spend the rest of his life with.

Matt was everything I had prayed for . . . and more.

He got down on one knee, presented me with a ring, and asked me to marry him. We exchanged vows eight and a half months later.

By now you're probably asking, "So now that you're married to the wonderful man God had in store for you . . . *what about sex?*" I get this question *all* the time!

THE WEDDING NIGHT

Some of you are afraid of your wedding night. I didn't realize that I was until it happened. I was so concerned with my wedding running smoothly and having everything perfect that I hadn't given much thought to what was going to happen once it was over. Our wedding was absolutely beautiful, and the reception was more than I had ever dreamed of. But

"I'M SCARED
TO HAVE SEX."

once our guests began leaving, I started getting nervous. I knew what was next on the agenda—and I knew that *everyone* else knew too!

Family and friends were telling us to just leave for our hotel; they would take care of the cleanup. My mom had already driven to the church to clean up there. Matt was ready to go—of course!—but I couldn't leave yet. Mom was supposed to be back at the reception hall soon, and I kept waiting for her to show up. I really needed to talk to her.

I waited for twenty more minutes, trying to look busy, but she still hadn't returned. She hadn't taken her cell phone with her, so I had no way to contact her. Finally I decided that I had to talk to someone else. I found my stepdad, Mark, up on a ladder, taking down big pink bows from the chandeliers.

"Dad, I need to talk to you," I said.

He immediately stepped down from the ladder and asked me what I needed to talk about.

I started to cry and said quietly, "I'm scared to have sex."

Like me, some survivors are afraid to have sex; others are repulsed by the mere thought of it. Still others use sex as a way to feel wanted, loved, or in control. All these responses are common, and all are ultimately damaging. If you grew up believing that what happened to you as a child is the way God intended sex to be, you're believing a lie that will have a disastrous effect on your marriage. That lie needs to be replaced with the truth of what God meant it to be like, so you can freely enjoy it when the time comes.

I already knew that God wants a husband and wife to thoroughly enjoy each other, and the Song of Songs is quite explicit that sex is a large part of that enjoyment. I wanted to enjoy marital intimacy as God intended me to. I wanted a good sex life. But in part because of my past abuse, on my wedding night I was afraid to have sex with my husband.

My stepdad put his arms around me and hugged me. I will never forget his calm, caring reaction or what he told me that night. He reminded me that I had married Matt because I loved him and he loved me. We cared about each other very much, we trusted each other, and we communicated well with each other. He said that it has to be the same way with regard to sex. He told me to tell Matt about my fears. He told me that it was important to talk to each other about it beforehand. And he told me to remember the person I was with: Matthew, my husband, the man God made for me.

My stepdad's words to me that night have stayed with both Matt and me to this day. I didn't want to talk to Matt about my fears that night, but after talking to my stepdad, I knew it was important, and I did share very deeply with him that night. Matt was so gentle and loving; I knew it would be okay.

THE MARRIAGE BED

With God's help, some abuse victims navigate dating relationships relatively easily and marry very caring, loving men. But later in the intimacy of the marriage bed, problems arise. Some women don't enjoy sex; there's no passion. They do it only to "get it over with." In some cases, married women become frigid and aren't able to have sex at all.

When we've been sexually abused, intimacy is often the last area in which we find complete healing. Even as we're finding freedom in other areas of our life, this one can take some time and a lot of work. Once you begin working on healing your memories of sexual abuse, everything can become harder, but this is especially true in the area of intimacy. Be prepared for that. It's normal. Things might get worse before they get better.

Just remember that you're not making a mistake in dealing with the pain of your past. Don't listen to Satan telling you that you shouldn't have faced it, or that it would be easier if you just continued to hide it away. He is a liar. The Word says that the truth will set you free. Even if it hurts and takes time, the truth will ultimately set you free.

Intimacy and sex can trigger issues you thought were settled. One slight movement or touch similar to something your abuser did can send your mind right back to that place in childhood. Triggers can happen at any time, but the emotions they cause are especially difficult during sexual intimacy. I think I have the greatest husband in the world. Yet painful memories can still come up during moments of intimacy. I want you to know that this is also normal.

My friend April asked her husband to switch his brand of deodorant when she finally realized that it reminded her of how her stepfather smelled when he had abused her during her childhood. This was causing her to shut down during moments of intimacy with her husband. Her husband thought it was something he was doing wrong, and she felt like a failure. Identifying the reason for her behavior brought healing and made their sex life enjoyable, as it was intended to be.

INTIMACY AND SEX CAN TRIGGER ISSUES YOU THOUGHT WERE SETTLED.

Overcoming your triggers will take a conscious effort at first. Sometimes you'll have to force your mind to stay in the present. Remind yourself where you are, how old you are, and whom you're with. Communicate with your spouse before, during, and after sexual intimacy. Share your feelings, thoughts, and concerns. Matt asks me all the time if I'm okay. He makes me remember that *I* am what is most important to him—not sex.

You need reassurance that you're safe and that your feelings matter. Tell your husband that you need to know you're okay. If you work on all these things and communicate with each other, you'll get stronger and stronger in the area of intimacy. Eventually, as healing takes place, it will become easier and easier to stay in the present moment. But again, it takes work. You have to be committed to this work in order to experience the reward of freedom.

Don't accept the lie that there is something totally wrong with you if sex is sometimes difficult. Don't be defeated and allow yourself to feel like a failure if you fear being intimate with your husband or if you don't enjoy sex. At the same time, don't think that you have to settle for an inadequate sex life with your husband. Jesus came so you could have life in abundance, and He means that in all areas of your life. Continue to seek the Lord about it, and talk with those whom He has sent you to for healing. With time and work, your triggers will be less likely to occur.

I have found that living with my fears brings me more hurt and chaos than facing them and trusting the Lord to help me overcome them. This has even happened in my marriage bed. Jesus makes all things new, and He can heal and transform this area of your life as well. He wants to give you the desires of your heart!

GOD IS OUR MERCIFUL FATHER AND THE SOURCE OF ALL COMFORT. HE COMFORTS US IN ALL OUR TROUBLES SO THAT WE CAN COMFORT OTHERS WHEN THEY ARE TROUBLED,

WE WILL BE ABLE TO GIVE THEM THE SAME COMFORT GOD HAS GIVEN US.

11

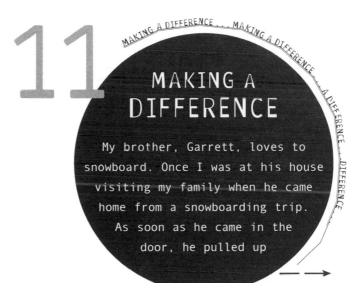

MAKING A
DIFFERENCE

My brother, Garrett, loves to snowboard. Once I was at his house visiting my family when he came home from a snowboarding trip. As soon as he came in the door, he pulled up

$\longrightarrow$

GOD IS OUR MERCIFUL FATHER

AND THE SOURCE OF ALL COMFORT.

HE COMFORTS US IN ALL OUR

TROUBLES SO THAT WE CAN COMFORT

OTHERS WHEN THEY ARE TROUBLED,

WE WILL BE ABLE TO GIVE THEM THE SAME

COMFORT GOD HAS GIVEN US.

2 Corinthians 1:3–4

his shirtsleeve to reveal a gaping wound from a collision with one of his buddies. His friend's board had sliced right through his coat, two shirts, and into his arm. Garrett still has the scars to prove it. Not only that, but he's proud of them!

I think we should approach our scars from sexual abuse in much the same way. When God heals our emotional wounds, we have a testimony of hope and of healing that we should be proud of. Just as Garrett shows people his physical scars, we have to show people our emotional scars—not because we think they're *cool*, but because of the glory the healing brings to God and the hope it brings others that their wounds will heal as well.

FIND your CALLING

In the summer of 1995, just before my fifteenth birthday, I went to church camp. It had been almost eleven months since my stepfather had committed suicide, and I had kept my vow of never telling my peers my secret. At the time, none of my friends at school or in my youth group knew.

On the last day of camp, the speaker recapped the messages he had given that week. Then he offered the mic to anyone who wanted to share a verse or testimony. I don't know how I ended up behind the microphone that Friday morning. Somehow my legs took me to the front of a huge group of teens from youth groups across our district, youth pastors, the college worship team, camp staff—and the really cute boy I had tried to sit next to all week during campfires! In front of all of them, I told my story. The moment I sat back down, I couldn't believe what I had just done. It was very quiet in the chapel pavilion. I thought maybe everybody was in shock.

The final events proceeded as scheduled, and we went through the normal end-of-camp routine. Girls comforted other girls who had to leave their "boyfriends" after a five-day romance, and we all exchanged addresses so we could write to our new friends. As we were packing up the church van, one of the girls I'd bonded with on the first day of camp approached me. It was my friend Raquel.

"A few years after my abuse occurred, I went to church camp and met Nicole," Raquel remembers. "We were the same age and had a lot of the same interests and immediately became friends. We hung out the entire week and developed a strong bond of friendship. But this bond wouldn't have been as significant if it weren't for what happened the last day of camp. During a time of open testimony in the morning chapel, Nicole told her story to all of us. I was amazed. I thought I was the only one. I was very nervous, but about ten minutes before my church's bus was to leave the campground, I told Nicole my secret. I had never told anyone before. We kept in touch that summer, and with the help of Nicole's letters of encouragement, I eventually told my family."

Raquel was the first to respond to my story, but not the last. After I'd been back home for a couple of weeks, the letters started coming . . . and they kept coming. I heard from teens who thanked me for having the courage to tell my story, and many of them shared their own story of sexual abuse for the first time. By telling my story, I had given others the courage to tell theirs. I wrote them back and began to pray for them. At fifteen, I was helping other victims of sexual abuse.

I began a daily routine of journaling and reading the Word. That's when the Lord led me to 2 Corinthians 1:3–4. Through these verses, God showed me my purpose. It was so real to me. It was like a flaming dagger piercing my heart, igniting a fire that couldn't be extinguished. I had to help more kids. I had to do whatever I could to comfort them, just as Christ had comforted me. God had called me to be a *voice*, and as I spoke up about sexual abuse, He used me to comfort others and set captives free.

As a young teenager, Lily had felt a clear call to ministry, but she couldn't reconcile her call with her history of sexual abuse. "I tried so hard to hide the abuse of my past," she says. "I was afraid I would be seen as tainted, broken, and unusable by God. Then one day Nicole came to speak at our Christian college. As she told her story, I realized that if *she* could stand up there in front of hundreds of people and share her story of abuse and inner healing, there must be hope for freedom. I told God that I would share *my* story if He would set *me* free too."

God did set Lily free. Through Christian counseling, He showed her that she needed to "go back" with Him and allow Him to comfort the little girl inside her who had been used, abused, and left confused and alone to fend for herself. God had placed a calling on her life when she was a little girl—to go and share the comfort of Jesus with those who have never known Him—but first she needed to experience His comfort for herself.

PURSUE YOUR PASSION

When God calls you, He plants a passion for your calling deep within your heart. The kind of passion I'm talking about is an intense desire to make a difference, to bring change, to do good in the lives of others. When I was a teenager, I cared deeply about victims of sexual abuse. It was a passion that had developed throughout my life *because* of my childhood.

I wanted to save children from abuse, but I thought it was too much for me to take on. *I'm only a five-foot-four girl from a small, country bumpkin town in Ohio,* I thought. *What can I do?* But as time went by, I found myself asking, *What can't I do? I may be small, but I have a voice, I have a passion to make a difference, and I have a God who has a purpose for my life. Those things can take me anywhere.* The apostle Paul said, "I can do everything through Christ, who gives me strength" (Philippians 4:13), and I came to believe that.

My passion is to bring hope to those who have been through the tragedy of sexual abuse. Traveling across the country, sharing my story to thousands of students, educating people to the fact that sexual abuse is everywhere, encouraging them to find their voices and speak out, to heal, to reach out to others, and to make a difference—that is my passion! And I discovered it by allowing God to comfort me in the midst of my troubles.

Let me be clear: I don't believe that God causes the pain we experience as survivors of abuse. He didn't make our abuse happen just so we could help others. *No.* But I do believe that the evil in this world is never so bad that God can't use it to make our life into something beautiful. Paul says, "In all things God works for the good of those who love him, who have been called according to his purpose" (Romans 8:28 NIV). He can make the problems of our lives seem meaningless compared to the good we can do because of them.

Paul also says that God "has created us anew in Christ Jesus, so we can do the good things he planned for us long ago" (Ephesians 2:10). Serving others by comforting them with the comfort God has given us is part of the good works He planned for us to do before we were even born. It's what enables us to find our callings, pursue our passions, and make a difference in the lives of others.

PRAY. DREAM. ASK THE LORD TO AWAKEN A PASSION INSIDE OF YOU.

Lily told me that God had begun moving in her life in a whole new way the day I spoke in chapel at her school. After my talk she had removed her mask, told her secret, and begun to heal from sexual abuse. Then God had placed a call on her heart to reach into Asia and help rescue children whose own families had sold them into prostitution.

"When God wove a new thread into my life in Asia," Lily says, "I began to understand why He allowed abuse to occur in my youth. If I hadn't received the comfort of my Father, there would be no way I could now minister comfort or encouragement or genuine love to these young girls. He truly does work all things out for the good of those who love Him and have been called according to His purpose.

"I'm not sure if we will ever be 100 percent unaffected by past abuse (until heaven), but God has shown me how crucial it is that I continue to experience His comfort, healing, and freedom in my life so I can minister to children on the other side of the world who need the same things. It's so important for survivors to fervently seek the intimate healing and comfort found in Jesus. You never know how many lives depend upon it."

Lily has a passion, one that is rooted in her experience. God has turned her broken life into something beautiful, and now she is drawing from the well of compassion she has received from the Lord and giving others a taste of His living water. She is making a difference.

What is your passion? You may feel as if you have little to no passion at all . . . about anything. You may feel you have nothing to give. Because you feel insignificant, you may think that God would not and will not call you to do anything important. You may be thinking that you have too much baggage for God to use you for good.

Lay all that aside. Pray. Dream. Ask the Lord to awaken a passion inside of you. Invite Him to reveal where He is calling you to serve. Trust Him with your future and His purpose for your life. God has gifted us all in a special way to fulfill a unique calling, and He assures us that His "gifts and his call can never be withdrawn" (Romans 11:29). He will never take our gifts away or change His mind about what He wants us to do with them. God has huge plans for you! The question is: Will you allow Him to carry them out?

Find your passion—something you believe in, something you're willing to sacrifice for, something you're willing to take risks for. And when people tell you that you've lost your mind, don't back down. Your passion will excite you! Your passion will engage you! It will keep you up at night, and it will get you out of bed in the morning!

LIVE OUT 2 CORINTHIANS 1:3-4

You've survived something awful, my friend. But you aren't alone. There are others out there who are going through the same thing right now. You may think you haven't received enough comfort yet to comfort them. But you have received some! You may think you have nothing to say. But you have a story! Whether you wanted to or not, you gained wisdom from your experience. Ask God to help you use it to serve others. Friend, if the Lord has called you out of the darkness into His light, comforted you, and healed you, then start talking! As you do, you'll experience more healing yourself.

It's true that we shouldn't get deeply involved in helping others heal when we still need to do some work on our own stuff. This could cause more problems in our own life, as well as in the lives of others. So don't jump in prematurely. But at the same time, don't wait too long or make excuses simply because you're afraid.

Satan wants you to believe that you aren't ready, and he already has some of you convinced. He doesn't want you to ever step out and help others, because that would mean setting captives free and bringing glory to God. Satan wants to trap you in the lie that you aren't good enough or strong enough, that you have no purpose or passion, and that you will never amount to anything. He wants you to focus on yourself and your pain to keep you from helping anyone else.

SATAN WANTS YOU TO BELIEVE THAT YOU AREN'T READY, AND HE ALREADY HAS SOME OF YOU CONVINCED.

People have a tough time believing that I'm a full-time speaker and an author. Quite honestly, I have a hard time believing it too! I hated speech class, and I don't have a PhD behind my name. But no excuse I can come up with is greater than God's call on my life to do whatever I can to comfort others, just as Christ has comforted me. I refuse to let excuses, fears, or Satan's attacks hold me back. What motivates me is just knowing that I am fulfilling God's purpose for my life by doing what He's given me a passion to do.

What excuses are holding you back from finding and fulfilling your calling and passion? Are you weak? Great! God will work through your weaknesses and use you because of it. Paul had a "thorn in the flesh" that made him feel weak. But when he asked God to remove it, the Lord said, "My grace is all you need. My power works best in weakness."

Paul got the message. "So now I am glad to boast about my weaknesses," he said, "so that the power of Christ can work through me" (2 Corinthians 12:9). All God asks is for you to be willing. All He asks is for you to say yes. He is asking: "Whom shall I send?" I pray you'll answer as Isaiah did. "Here am I. Send me!" (Isaiah 6:8 NIV).

You *do* have something to give. So give it! Give to those who have nothing. Give to those who don't know yet that they deserve better. Speak truth to those who believe the lies you once believed. Comfort those who mourn, as you once mourned so deeply. Tell others that it wasn't their fault, just as you once needed to hear those words over and over again. Offer your compassion, just as you have received compassion. Accept her. Pray for him. Encourage them. Love in all the ways God has loved you. You may feel you don't have much to give, but what you do have may be exactly what someone else is desperately searching for.

is the overflow of personal healing.

God asks us to reach out to others in whatever way we can. He says that whatever we do for the least, the last, or the lost, we are doing for Him; whatever we do not do for them, we do not do for Him (Matthew 25:35–40). You might not be called to be a public speaker like me. You may not be called to a foreign country like Lily. But no matter where you are, or what your profession is, you are surrounded by hurting people. What can you do? You can empathize with their pain. You can provide a safe place for them to share their fears or their story.

If you're a doctor or nurse, you can teach yourself to watch for signs of sexual abuse in your patients, and then follow through by reporting your suspicions. If you're a teacher, you can do the same for your students. If you work in a clothing or grocery store, you can be alert to customers who show signs of depression or abuse. Maybe you and a few friends go to the dollar theater on a Friday night, and as you pass a bag of Gummy Bears down the row a scene depicting sexual abuse flashes across the screen. Will you be brave enough to say something once the movie is over? These are opportunities. Don't miss them! Victims who are silently hurting are waiting for you to speak up and reach out.

Living out 2 Corinthians 1:3–4 can mean comforting abuse victims, but it can also mean just speaking an encouraging word to a coworker who has had a recent death in the family, or a child having a hard time in school, or a woman at church who has shared about her relationship problems, or a high school girl who struggles with body image. You are called to comfort *anyone* going through *anything* because of the comfort you have already received.

REACH OUT

Our steps toward healing and freedom from our pain mean very little if they don't lead us to a place of service. God asks that we give to others from what He has given us. When you allow God to come into your dark closet and heal the wounded places within you, you can be a blessing in that area to others. His healing waters have showered you, and you now have a well for others to draw from.

Ministry to others is the overflow of personal healing. If you aren't seeking ways to reach your hand out to help someone, as God has done for you, you've missed out on a big chunk of healing. You heal when you use what you have received to help others find healing. This is the fourth step in moving from silence to healing. In my opinion, we aren't truly healed if we aren't helping others.

Want to walk in the freedom and the love and the healing and the comfort you have received? Want to go beyond the call of duty and find an even greater meaning and purpose to your life? I do. I don't want to simply survive. Like Garrett, I want to live on the edge. Sure, he gets hurt sometimes; but when he does, he brushes himself off, learns from his experiences, and gets right back out there as he strives to reach his goals.

I hope you'll choose to do your part to make a difference by comforting others with the comfort you yourself have received. Choosing to not reach out builds a dam that holds back the healing waters in your life. Meeting the needs of others may not always be the easiest or most fun thing to do, but when you serve in the name of Christ, God will strengthen and reward you.

I often find myself completely drained after speaking on a college campus. But when I see the lightbulbs come on in hearts and minds during meetings with students, and when I read the e-mails I receive from them, I feel power flowing in my veins. Giving others the comfort, love, acceptance, and compassion that God has given me gives me even more life than I had before. I have found that the more I give, the more I receive.

Lily's story and the stories of other young people I meet and keep in contact with bring me great joy. From their simple act of removing their masks the day I meet them, to keeping in touch with me as they move from silence to healing, I see God making their stories beautiful. Part of the beauty of their healing has been their passion to live out 2 Corinthians 1:3–4.

Finding God's calling and pursuing the passion He has given you means taking risks for the sake of others. I have taken many risks in getting to where I am right now. But it has all been worth it because I know I am making a difference in other people's lives. When you offer your life to Christ, He will love others through you. He will place people in your path who need the difference only you can make. Just be willing . . . they will come! Trust me on this.

Survivors tell me all the time that other survivors are drawn to them like magnets, without even knowing their story. Lily said that when she went to a Christian college, she quickly became friends with others like her—Christian girls with similar abuse in their past, struggling to understand its effects and find some kind of relief, comfort, and inner healing. This was true for me as well.

If I may tweak a line from *The Field of Dreams*, I would say, "If you *un*-build it, they will come." If you tear down the walls you've built to protect yourself, God will use you to bring down walls in the lives of others. Get ready! They will come!

THE
HEALING
JOURNEY

I've always pictured the healing journey as a long dark tunnel with a light at the end. At first I could barely see the pinpoint of light in the distance, but with every step, the circle of light kept getting bigger and bigger. It was never enough for me to clearly see what was ahead of me, but it was always enough to guide my next step forward. That is how healing was for me. Step by step, I was working my way toward the light.

Telling my secret was the first step in moving from silence to healing. To some, this may sound too simple; to others, it may sound too difficult. But for all of us, breaking the silence is vital and the place to begin.

After I told my story, I still struggled to believe that my abuse wasn't my fault. In fact, I struggled more with this false belief after I told than I did before. Accepting this truth was the second step to healing, and it was a huge hurdle for me. For a long time it kept me from experiencing freedom and wholeness. To destroy this powerful lie, I had to stand firm in the truth and in God's Word.

On my healing journey, I also had to stay connected with people who could support me. Good mentors and counselors helped me work through the pain, fear, anger, sadness, guilt, shame, confusion, and other emotions that surfaced along the way. But more importantly, I had to stay connected with God, for my relationship with Him was the true source of my healing. God is the Great Physician, the only One with all the answers to our healing. Admitting our need for Him and allowing Him to help us day by day keeps us moving in the right direction.

As you journey through the tunnel of healing, there will be days where the light at the end will seem dim and freedom a long way off. I encourage you to keep pressing on in spite of those days. Trust me; they aren't the end of your story. When you feel overwhelmed, slow down. Remember, it takes time to heal. Take it a day at a time or even a minute at a time. Take baby steps, and don't look too far ahead. Little things mean a lot on the road to recovery. Whatever you do, don't give up! Move forward in spite of your doubts and fears and anguish. There are brighter days ahead; but if you stop moving, you'll never find them.

Everyone's journey will look a little different; some will be very unique. There is no precise agenda for bringing everyone into the light at the end of the tunnel. But one thing is certain: Forgiveness is a huge step in taking you to that place of freedom. It is the third major step to healing.

Forgiveness can be something that happens one time, or it may need to happen many times. You may find that you'll need to forgive many people, including yourself, over and over until you are convinced that forgiveness is complete. Forgive those who hurt you. Forgive yourself. If you've wronged someone else, confess your sins to the Lord and ask Him to forgive you. Be patient along the way as God reveals the people you need to forgive.

Cling to God's hand, follow His lead, and allow Him to heal you. Before you know it, you'll be nearing the end of the dark tunnel and the freedom found in that light up ahead. Keep looking at the light and keep walking, my friend. As you do, you'll be able to use the comfort you've received along the way to help others. Grab hold of God's purpose for your life and reach out to others. When you do, you take the fourth major step on your healing journey.

Are you still sitting in a dark closet crammed full of old issues and pain? If you are, Satan has you just where he wants you. He hopes you'll never tell your story, never believe the abuse wasn't your fault, never forgive, and never make a difference in the lives of others. Or are you sorting things out and no longer worried about things falling out for others to see? If so, will you risk opening that closet door and stepping out on your healing journey?

Some of you don't want to take even one step into that tunnel. But believe me, unless you do, you won't experience the freedom waiting for you at the end. There's no way around it. To get to the light, you can only go *through* the tunnel.

I write to you as one who understands the importance of facing my fears, getting up, and crawling out of a dark closet filled with painful memories. Once I began my healing journey, I was able to make a difference in an unsafe world for the sake of others and for the glory of God. I invite those of you who have walked in my shoes to continue this journey with me. When you do, the momentum will build.

As more and more of us move toward healing and invite others to take this journey with us, we'll become part of a greater movement. We'll experience the joy and satisfaction of moving together toward a campus, a community, a nation, and a world healing from sexual abuse. God's mission will be accomplished through me, through you, and through those yet to come. As more of us choose the path of healing today, fewer children will be victimized tomorrow.

Today is moving day! Move out of your tiny closet of pain and shame, and begin the journey that will bring good out of the evil that Satan meant for your destruction. Carry with you the things that matter; leave behind the fears and addictions that kept you feeling trapped, isolated, and dead. The road to freedom lies directly in front of you. All you need to do is take the first step toward the light.

NO MORE
SECRETS

My purpose in writing <u>Hush</u> has been to reveal the truth about sexual abuse, to help you find your voice, and to give you hope that you too can move from silence to healing. I hope I have achieved that goal.

Know that I'm praying for you and for every other person who picks up this book. I'm praying that the little child inside of you—the one who was hurt and confused and not allowed to tell—will know that it's now safe to come out, break the silence, and begin to heal.

Remember, you don't have to go it alone. I encourage you to find a good Christian counselor who can walk with you on your healing journey, and to take advantage of the hotlines and other resources available to you along the way. Here are just a few to help you get started:

If you suspect that a child is being abused or neglected, you should call your local child protective services agency or the agency in the county or state in which the abuse occurred. To get help finding the appropriate agency number, or to speak with a crisis counselor, contact: Childhelp USA National Child Abuse Hotline. This anonymous hotline is dedicated to the prevention of both sexual and nonsexual child abuse. Staffed twenty-four hours a day by professional crisis counselors, the hotline provides crisis counseling, referrals, research, and educational curricula. Translators are available. Call 1-800-4-A-CHILD (1-800-422-4453) or 1-800-2-A CHILD (TDD line) or go to their Web site at http://www.child-helpusa.org.

The Rape, Abuse, and Incest National Network (RAINN) is an organization that operates America's only twenty-four hour confidential national phone hotline for survivors of sexual assault. Call 1-800-656-HOPE (1-800-656-4673) or go to their new online hotline at www.rainn.org. This is a secure Web-based crisis hotline that provides live, completely confidential help to victims through instant messaging. Victims who need help but are reluctant to call the telephone hotline have the option of communicating securely online with someone trained to help them take steps toward recovery.

The National Domestic Violence Hotline (NDVH) offers callers help twenty-four hours a day, 365 days a year. For victims and anyone calling on their behalf, advocates are available to provide crisis intervention, safety planning, information, and referrals to agencies in all fifty states, Puerto Rico, and the U.S. Virgin Islands. Assistance is available in English and Spanish, with access to more than 140 languages through interpreter services. If you or someone you know is frightened about something in any of your relationships, call the NDVH at 1-800-799-SAFE (7233) or 1-800-787-3224 (TTY).

The National Hopeline Network brings the tremendous knowledge, skill, and resources of existing crisis centers under the umbrella of a single, easy-to-remember, toll-free telephone number. The Hopeline Network makes appropriate, critical services available to everyone. Call 1-800-SUICIDE(1-800-784-2433) or go online at http://www.hopeline.com.

The National Sexual Violence Resource Center (NSVRC) is a comprehensive collection and distribution center for information, research, and emerging policy on sexual violence intervention and prevention. In addition to coordinating National Sexual Assault Awareness Month initiatives, it provides an extensive online library and customized technical assistance. Go to http://www.nsvrc.org.

The National Center of Missing and Exploited Children is the nation's resource center for child protection. It assists parents, children, law enforcement agencies, schools, and the community in recovering missing children and raising public awareness about ways to help prevent child abduction, molestation, and sexual exploitation. Call 1-800-THE-LOST (1-800-843-5678) or go online at http://www.missingkids.com.

The Federal Bureau of Investigation offers a resource to parents on how to protect children from online predators. It is called "A Parent's Guide to Internet Safety" and is found at http://www.fbi.gov/publications/pguide/pguidee.htm.

The National Center for Victims of Crime is dedicated to forging a national commitment to help victims of crime rebuild their lives. Their toll-free help line offers supportive counseling, practical information about crime and victimization, and referrals to local community resources, as well as skilled advocacy in the criminal justice and social service systems. Their help line number is 1-800-FYI-CALL (1-800-394-2255).

Victims of Pornography is a project sponsored by Citizens for Community Values (http://www.ccv.org). It is designed to help our society realize that pornography is not victimless, that it is affecting our families and friends, and that recognizing this fact is the key to changing lives. Go to http://www.victimsofpornography.org.

OneVOICE enterprises is an organization committed to raising awareness of sexual violence, creating a national platform for sexual abuse prevention, pointing students toward healthy lifestyle and relationship choices, and empowering people to make a difference as they journey from victim to "Victory Over Impossible CircumstancEs." For more information, go online to http://www.onevoice enterprises.com.

ABOUT THE AUTHOR

Nicole Braddock Bromley is a full-time professional speaker who travels across America speaking on sexual abuse, harassment, and assault. She presents her nationally recognized keynote program "Our Little Secret" to thousands of students each year at colleges, high schools, middle schools, churches, residential treatment centers, and conferences.

Nicole's work has gained her media attention, and she has appeared in magazines and newspapers and on television and radio broadcasts. She is a featured author in <u>Chicken Soup for the Recovering Soul: Daily Inspirations</u> (2006). She is also the founder and director of OneVOICE enterprises, an organization dedicated to making a difference in the lives of survivors of abuse, one day at a time.

Nicole and her husband, Matthew, live in Columbus, Ohio. You can reach her at www.onevoiceenterprises.com.

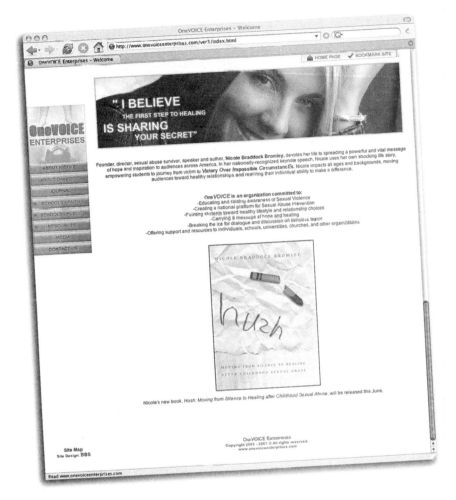

Need more help and information?
Come visit Nicole at her Web site:

www.OneVOICEenterprises.com

Weights that wear you down,
Weights that refine,
Qualified for the climb

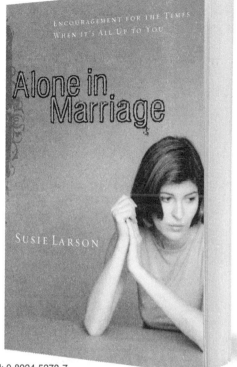

ISBN: 0-8024-5278-7
ISBN-13: 978-0-8024-5278-8

Often when a woman ends up carrying the weight of the marriage (due to factors such as her husband's health, choices, workload), her tendency is to "get out or check out." She may consider her husband's distraction an opportunity to do her own thing. But is there a better way to walk through this season? Even thrive? Susie Larson stands in as an encouraging friend, walking with you, helping you to discern how anxiety and anger will slow you down; and how loneliness and disappointment can actually refine and bless you. You will be challenged and inspired as you realize that God has His arms around you.

by Susie Larson
Find it now at your favorite local or online bookstore.
www.MoodyPublishers.com

Bringing your hurts to the One who can help

ISBN: 0-8024-4600-0
ISBN-13: 978-0-8024-4600-8

Jennifer Kennedy Dean is an intercessor who has experienced the healing power of prayer. In *When You Hurt and When He Heals*, Jennifer guides you through a series of meditations designed to encourage and challenge you as you put your life in the hands of almighty God, and allow Him to heal you—physically, emotionally, mentally, and spiritually.

by Jennifer Kennedy Dean
Find it now at your favorite local or online bookstore.
www.MoodyPublishers.com

God uses the most horrible situations . . . and the most unlikely messengers.

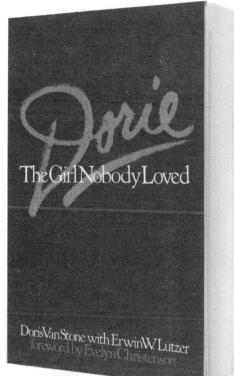

ISBN: 0-8024-2275-6
ISBN-13: 978-0-8024-2275-0

As a child, Dorie was rejected by her mother, sent to live in an orphanage where she was regularly beaten by the orphanage director, was beaten time and again by cruel foster parents, and was daily told that she was ugly and unlovable. Dorie never knew love until a group of college students visited the orphanage and told her that God loved her. As she accepted that love, her life began to change. *Dorie* is the thrilling, true account of what God's love can do in a life.

No Place to Cry is available as the sequel to *Dorie*.

by Doris Van Stone and Erwin W. Lutzer
Find it now at your favorite local or online bookstore.
www.MoodyPublishers.com

What Schools Say about the Message of *Hush*:

Nicole gave a wonderfully poised and important talk. She is a naturally engaging speaker and her humor and humanity does wonders in helping the audience face the nature of this issue. She clearly connected with our students, and the dialogue on the topic continued in classes and informally between friends. The awareness that Nicole raises is invaluable, but most importantly she is a life ring to those out there who she quite accurately notes are suffering silently.

~ Mike Gengras, Asst. Dean of Students
North Yarmouth Academy, ME

Nicole Braddock Bromley is a conscientious person who is not afraid to discuss sensitive and complex sexual issues/concerns. She models and expects professionalism, and takes her responsibilities for sexual assault education and prevention very seriously. She also exhibits a great sense of humor and encourages an open exchange of ideas and solutions in her presentations. I feel extremely honored to recommend Nicole Braddock Bromley to you with the highest of enthusiasm.

~ Kimberly M. Ferguson, Associate Dean of Students & Director of Judicial Affairs,
Capital University, OH

In 25 years of working with Christian University Chapel speakers, I can count on one hand the number of women who have touched the hearts of students the way Nicole Bromley did during her visit. The way Lori Salierno can challenge students to go beyond their comfort zone and serve the Lord, Nicole can bring students to that place in their personal lives where they are ready for that challenge. Speaking out of incredible authenticity, with compassion, clarity, sensitivity, and grace, Nicole opened up damaged hearts with the skill of a surgeon and brought a powerful word of hope and peace in Jesus Christ. If I can have her back to Spring Arbor every year, I will. Christian University students NEED to hear Nicole Braddock Bromley.

~ Ron Kopicko, University Chaplain
Spring Arbor University, MI

Nicole impacted our students tremendously. Our counselor was inundated with students seeking help after her message. It is a difficult topic, but one that obviously needs to be dealt with, and she did so with candor and vulnerability. Her presentation was tasteful, appropriate, informative, and gripping—the chapel has never been so silent for a speaker. Nicole had the students with her the entire time.

~ Carl Creedon, Campus Pastor/Associate Dean of Students
San Diego Christian College, CA

100636